Motorbooks International Illustrated Buyer's Guide Series

Illustrated

Studebaker

BUYER'S ★ GUIDE ™

Richard M. Langworth

Motorbooks International
Publishers & Wholesalers

To the memory of
Louis F. B. Carini,
a friend

First published in 1991 by Motorbooks International Publishers & Wholesalers, P O Box 2, 729 Prospect Avenue, Osceola, WI 54020 USA

© Richard M. Langworth, 1991

Motorbooks International is a certified trademark, registered with the United States Patent Office

Motorbooks International books are also available at discounts in bulk quantity for industrial or sales-promotional use. For details write to Special Sales Manager at the Publisher's address

Library of Congress Cataloging-in-Publication Data
Langworth, Richard M.
    Illustrated Studebaker buyer's guide / Richard M. Langworth.
        p.   cm. -- (Motorbooks International illustrated buyer's guide series)
    Includes bibliographical references.
    ISBN 0-87938-490-5
    1. Studebaker automobile—Purchasing.   2. Studebaker automobile—Collectors and collecting.   I. Title.   II. Title: Studebaker buyer's guide.   III. Series.
TL215.S79L36 1991   90-13312
629.22'2--dc20   CIP

On the front cover: The great 1957 Studebaker Golden Hawk designed by Bob Bourke. This car is owned by Bob Patrick. *Bud Juneau*

On the back cover: Sixty years of Studebaker, from the early Electric to the Avanti.

Printed and bound in the United States of America

Contents

Acknowledgments

The book would not have been possible without the collaboration and technical advice of my friend Asa Hall, with whom I have worked before on our photo documentary *The Studebaker Century* (Dragonwyck Publishing Inc.). Hall's mammoth collection supplied most of the photographs herein. He worked with me on the appraisals and summaries for many chapters and on the appendix on postwar problem areas.

I should like to thank Michael Dregni, Barbara Harold, the editorial staff of Motorbooks International and the countless members of the Studebaker Drivers Club who provided information and experiences. I should also like to thank George D. Krem and Fred Fox for their Avanti information.

Introduction

Studebaker has had a bum rap.

I don't mean from the vacant boffins of the electronic news media, who live in New York and Washington, D. C., where cars are hazardous, polluting noisemakers and who won't accept the idea that real people also live in other places. It's true, of course, that poor old Studebaker doesn't fare well at *their* hands: the same dummkopfs who tried to pillory a responsible company named Audi for the ignorance of drivers who stepped on the wrong pedal and found themselves in "unintended acceleration" will trot out Studebaker as a symbol of all that's funny or futile about cars. "I once owned a Studebaker" is supposed to tickle your funny bone at least as well as "I once owned an Edsel."

But it's worse than that. Studebaker has had a bum rap from people who are expected to know better: those fume-breathing, grease-covered, chrome-happy, gas-in-the-blood barbarians known as car collectors. Us.

Granted, Studebaker is an easy target. We know that its management, after the war, did so many foolish things all at once that, had they purposely set out to sink the company within twenty years, they couldn't have gone about it in a more efficient way. Some of its cars were, let's face it, pretty laughable too. So for people incapable of complex thought, it's all too easy to sweep the whole subject into history's dustbin, dismissing every Studebaker as a non-car and those who drive them as nutballs and hayseeds.

Rational analysis of the product shows that Studebaker built about the same proportion of good and bad cars as everybody else, including the still-surviving makes, and at least as many truly outstanding cars as most of them. The Studebaker Garfords of the dawning age of motoring were among the best of the horseless carriages; the 30 and 40 hp models are among the most desirable antiques today. The Studebaker Electrics were the most successful application of electric power to production automobiles in history—and that includes history right up to the present day. The Studebaker President was one of the most glorious cars of the Golden Age and set countless records on road and track. It was also beautifully styled, impeccably engineered, and a better road car than such highly respected Classics (by definition of the Classic Car Club of America) as Packard, Cadillac and Pierce-Arrow. And I have this on the authority of people who have owned all four.

Not only the President, but the Commanders and Dictators designed in its image, were sterling performers capable of setting remarkable endurance and speed records, each in their class, on venues as diverse as Brooklands and Indianapolis, the transcontinental trek and Atlantic City's boardtracks. The 1939 Champion was arguably a better economy car than anything from the Big Three, and the 1947 models introduced America to genuine postwar styling two years before the Big Three did. The 1953

Starliner and Starlight coupes were by far the most brilliant expression of American industrial design on any car of the 1950s, so well proportioned that they don't look their age even today. The Hawks, which grew from them, were America's first real pony cars, and the Gran Turismo Hawk of 1962 was dollar for dollar the most successful facelift ever conceived on a ten-year-old body.

Against all this one need hardly mention the Avanti, a car that blew every bucket-seat Detroit sedan out of the water in its day, set scores of speed records and remains in production as I write—the only "replicar" based on such a young design.

This razzing we've all given Studebaker over the years (and I've done my share) really deserves to be laid aside. We are dealing here with an interesting subject: an example, in many cases, of American design and engineering at its best, and withal, a make of car that deserves to be preserved and remembered. Furthermore, and somewhat contrary to contemporary currents, Studebakers are not zooming out of sight nor are they spurred on by frequent appearances at auctions, where the wealthy are known to spend double what a car is worth, or dealers to sell cars back and forth to each other at higher and higher prices until a customer comes along and takes it off their happy hands. The result: a body of cars that can be historically important, fun to drive and own, and not so expensive as to require a second mortgage.

This Buyer's Guide covers every model from the Studebaker-Garfords through the line of light- and heavy-duty trucks to today's Avanti—not because they're all available (far from it), but because I thought they all deserve consideration. Buying a Studebaker, at least from the prewar era, is largely a matter of opportunity: you may set out seeking the elegant 1932 President St. Regis brougham, but find a junior-edition Dictator in a condition or at a price that makes it just about irresistible. You can count Studebaker Fours on one, maybe two hands—but that doesn't mean another one might not surface tomorrow. In areas where there's a wide choice (Larks or Land Cruisers, for exam-

ple), I have tried to channel my comments so as to cover the pros and cons of various models and years.

Chapters otherwise follow the Buyer's Guide format: a backgrounder; some remarks on what to look for (conditions, special models, peculiar maladies); production figures by model year; identification; and specifications. Where possible, I also include serial number listings. With forgeries and fakes a fact of life in the old car avocation these days, I thought it important to state the factory's serial number spans for potential buyers. For the serial numbers I acknowledge four excellent sources: the National Automobile Dealers Association (NADA) and *Red Book* used car value guides published over the years; Fred Fox's and Bill Cannon's model history, *Studebaker—The Complete Story* (Tab Books, 1981); and the *Standard Catalogues of American Cars* covering 1805–1942 (Krause Publications, 1985) and 1946–1975 (second revised edition, Krause, 1987).

Investment Ratings

I so much enjoyed Graham Arnold's *Illustrated Lotus Buyer's Guide* that I determined to structure my own investment ratings along the same lines. Arnold made his book entertaining, a work to be enjoyed by the nonspecialist as well as the marque nut. With this in mind, I have adopted his rating system, looking at the fun, investment and anguish of owning a specified model.

It occurred to me that the traditional one-to five-star rating system used in a Buyer's Guide was fairly imprecise, not broadly indicative of a car's character. An R3 Avanti is great fun and a prime investment, for example, and would get five stars in the old system, but tune-ups will be frequent and some engine parts impossible to find. A star rating would not reveal this, but a 9 in the anguish column is more suggestive. (On the other hand, a conventional R1 Avanti rates 8 for fun and investment, only 5 for anguish.)

To give another example, the between-wars Dictator rates a steady 4 in the anguish column, but open bodies and the St. Regis brougham rate 7 as investments, against only 2 or 3 for the other Dictator models;

however, the St. Regis rates only 4 for fun compared to a 6 for the open bodies.

In the *Illustrated Lotus Buyer's Guide* the anguish factor was defined as reflecting two aspects of ownership: "first, the likelihood of outright failure and frequency of nagging faults; and second, the shortage of spare parts and/or information, even sympathy." I have adopted that definition wholesale!

This rating system remains imprecise, as all rating systems are; but it's far more revealing than the star system. I like it, and hope you will find it useful.

Price History

Value guides are a controversial subject among collectors. There are those who believe cars should never be represented in print by columns of filthy lucre—that dollar values have no place in old car publications. Others insist that price and value are intrinsic to the subject and cannot be ignored.

As enthusiasts we primarily love the cars in their own right as cars, and we are not interested in parlaying them into profits like a stock portfolio. But the days when we all owned a lot of cars, and played with them all for relatively little money, are over. Today the old car collecting field has become a big business. The typical old car collection has shrunk dramatically, and the entry level is so forbidding that newcomers often can afford only one car. Whether we are one-car collectors or owners of stables, however, we thus have to take notice of the financial angle.

There are now financial newsletters for car collectors which make predictions of future values, an effort to explain what's going up and what's not over the next year, or five years, or ten years. A Buyer's Guide, however, is a book, not a periodical. It cannot possibly be as up-to-the-minute. But it *can* say where a car has *been*, in terms of value, as a permanent reference point for the collector.

Thus I decided to present here the price history of show-quality cars over the past eight years: specifically, the approximate high price of each model in 1982, 1987 and 1990. I have also calculated the compound annual rate of return on those figures, as if they'd been invested in a certificate of deposit or a stock portfolio instead of in a car. Thus, for example, if you bought a 1927 Erskine roadster in prime condition for, say, $12,500 in 1982, and your car is worth $27,500 today, that represents a compound return rate of 10.4 percent, which is pretty good by today's interest rates.

But the conclusion requires qualifications. Cars are not CDs or stock portfolios; they require maintenance, insurance, parts and service. The price figures are highly arbitrary, taken from three or four sources and averaged. Prices apply only to very fine, condition 1 original or restored cars, which always command far more than the same models in mediocre condition.

It is not possible to measure individually the overhead involved in eight years' ownership of any specific car. Obviously, running costs and insurance are going to be higher for an Avanti, say, than a 1947 Champion business coupe. On the other hand, the compound rate of return does not take into consideration the intangible fun of ownership—which, after all, counts for something.

I like to say to myself: "Well, the costs of maintenance, insurance, garaging and so on are evenly balanced by the fun of ownership, so the two factors cancel each other out." This is perhaps too glib a statement, but it does point to one salient fact: the return figure is only a comparative guide to what the best examples of each model have sold for over the past eight years. Where the car is going in the future is up to you to decide, based on your own perceptions of the market.

Richard M. Langworth
Hopkinton, New Hampshire
October 1990

Chapter 1

Electrics 1902–10

Electrics	Fun	Investment	Anguish
	7	3	8

The Studebaker Electric obviously evolved from the buggies the firm had been building in the nineteenth century, though it gradually acquired more style and sophistication. From runabouts, traps and stanhopes in 1902, South Bend moved into closed cars, the most memorable of which was the winsome coupe of 1910–12. Much taller than it was wide, with thick plate glass and an elegant interior, the 1910 Electric coupe would trundle along at 15 mph, hardly up to even 1910 standards. But by then Studebaker was well along with its gasoline automobiles, much to the disgust of company president John M. "Wheelbarrow Johnny" Studebaker, whose opinion on the subject is deathless: Gasoline cars, Mr. J.M. said, were "clumsy, dangerous, noisy brutes [which] stink to high heaven, break down at the worst possible moment, and are a public nuisance."

John M. Studebaker (hand on tiller), toward the end of his life, with an Electric, which he always preferred to gasoline cars. The site is the elevated boardwalk at South Bend, said to have been Studebaker's first proving ground.

Four days before Studebaker's fiftieth anniversary, on February 12, 1902, it sold its first horseless carriage: an Electric runabout purchased by F.W. Blees of Macon, Missouri. A similar car appears in this drawing: Model 1354 with "stick seat."

The Studebaker Electric spanned the period of transition from motorized buggies to cars as we know them, the horseless carriage years of the early 1900s. In its lifetime spoke wheels gave way to artillery wheels, fenders grew and were connected by running boards. Tiller steering was apparently a characteristic of all models. "Noiseless, easy running, motor suspended above the springs, avoids all jarring," Studebaker ads claimed for the Electric. "Excels all other makes in the pleasure and comfort of occupants, prolongs the life of the machine and reduces cost of repairs. Run 40 miles with a single charging. Four rates of speed. Always ready, night or day."

What To Look For

Since the going price of an Electric seems to be no more than $20,000 (and that for the finest examples), and since the supply is low, defining items of special interest is an academic, and personal, exercise. Personally I think the Electric looks better with spoke rather than artillery wheels—spokes are more in line with its era. The most attractive body style is the single-seater stanhope, a "toy tonneau" with running boards and a canopy top. The most charming is the coupe, said to have originated as early as 1906. The most interesting are the Electric Delivery with its van body, which can be suitably decorated with period lettering, and the twin-motor commercial vehicles rated to carry up to an astonishing 7,500 lb.

Production

	1902–10
Electrics	1,841

Identification

Tiller steering, full-elliptic rear springs, Westinghouse electric motor, chain drive.

Specifications

Bodies: Runabout, stanhope, victoria (runabout with top); coupe and phaeton from 1906; twin-motor, four-passenger surrey (1905–06), plus commercial vehicles.

Engines: Westinghouse 24 cell, 40 volt electric motor (runabout); 24 cell, 50 volts, 36 cell optional (two-passenger models 1904–10); 40 cells, twin 40 volt motors (1904 surrey and commercials), 48 volts (coupe).

Chassis and drivetrain: Solid axles with semi-elliptic leaf springs front and full-elliptic leaf springs rear. Chain drive with four speeds forward and reverse. Solid tires (early models and surrey). Rear axle drum (wheel hubs on surrey) and motor countershaft brakes.

Dimensions: Wheelbase 61 to 70 in.; weight from 1,350 lb. (runabout) to 2,500 lb. (coupe), commercials up to 9,500 lb.

Price History

95+ point condition 1	1982	1987	1990	Return*
Electrics	$10,000	$15,000	$20,000	9.1%

*Eight-year compound annual rate of return for comparison purposes only, based strictly on high average prices unadjusted for upkeep, repairs and running costs.

Chapter 2

Studebaker-Garfield 1903–11

	Fun	Investment	Anguish
Touring, to 30 hp	5	4	7
Touring, 40 hp	7	7	7
Runabout, to 30 hp	8	7	7
Roadster, 40 hp	10	9	7
Closed models, to 30 hp	5	4	7
Closed models, 40 hp	7	7	7

The first gasoline cars were called Studebaker-Garfords because their chassis were built by the Garford Company of Elyria, Ohio, then shipped to South Bend for body and drivetrain assembly. Trade references to Garford Model As and Bs have been noted in some sources, but none are known to exist. The 1904 Model C 16 hp (NACC rated 8 hp) twin cylinder is considered the first gasoline-powered Studebaker. The twins gave way to a four-cylinder 20 hp during 1908. Garford Fours continued to be built through 1913, when Garford's assets were acquired by Willys-Overland. However, the Studebaker-Garford connection ended in 1911.

The 1904 Model C mounted its flat twin amidships on a sturdy ladder chassis with a wheelbase of 82 in. Featuring a two-speed gearbox and chain drive, it was variously labeled the Model C or Model 202, and continued, as the Model 9502, into 1905. It sold for $1,600, or $1,750 with canopy top.

In 1905 Studebaker launched a vertical four of much larger displacement and 28–30 hp. Confusingly, the T-head Garford of 1908 was dubbed Model B, but is better known by its horsepower rating as the Series 40. This fast, handsome and expensive car was available in various forms through 1911. Garfords were continued under their own name through 1913 and also briefly marketed under the Garford badge in 1908–09.

What To Look For

The oldest known Garford is a 1904 model, and it is the only one of its kind. Like Electrics, the question is not so much which Garford to choose but whether you can find one for sale. It does seem appropriate here to attempt to straighten out the confusing maze of Studebaker-Garford models.

Models A and B (1903–04). Opposed two-cylinder tonneau, also apparently offered with commercial bodies. None known to exist.

From the Studebaker archives, captioned "the first gasoline powered vehicle manufactured by the Studebaker brothers," a 1904 Garford touring. Only one 1904 is known to exist.

One of the most desirable Studebaker-Garfords is the 1910 G-7, with 40 hp vertical four and the longest wheelbase ever offered. Laden with brass, this is an impressive car.

Early Garford Fours, with the 20 hp 212 engine. Top, 1905 Model 9503, the first four-cylinder model, with touring body; bottom, 1906 Model E victoria.

Two more 40 hp verticals. Top, 1908 Model B touring; bottom, 1908 roadster, probably a Model H, the epitome of sporting motoring—it would be a great find today.

Model C (1904) and Model 9502 (1905). Opposed two-cylinder with rear- and side-entrance touring bodies. One 1904 model known.

Model 9503 (1905) and Model E (1906). Vertical four-cylinder with touring and town car bodies. Few known to exist.

Model F (1906), Model L (1907) and Model M (1910). Vertical four-cylinder with large, heavy, five-passenger touring body. Lots of brasswork on the Model L and M; nice if you can get one.

Model G (1906), Model H (1907-08 and 1910) and Model C (1909). Vertical four-cylinder with more luxurious touring body similar to but more elaborate and more desirable than the Model F.

Model A (1908–09). Vertical four-cylinder with touring, town car, runabout and landaulet bodies. Ranks with Model G above.

Model B, or Garford 40 (1908–09). Vertical four-cylinder, first of the big 40s, with touring, runabout, limousine, landaulet, tourabout and three-passenger "speed car" bodies. Has the desirable T-head engine, with cylinders cast in two blocks of two. Considered the best Garfords, commanding the highest prices, with the most sought after antique engine configuration, the widest original array of bodies and plenty of brass.

Model D (1909), G-7 (1910) and G-8 (1911). Vertical four-cylinder with touring body (Model D), four/five- and seven-passenger touring and limousine bodies (1910). Another 40 hp Garford, with the longest wheelbase ever offered. Highly desirable.

Model G-10 (1911). Vertical four-cylinder with five-passenger touring body. Relatively long wheelbase but 30 hp engine only. Probably found with Studebaker badges only.

Identification

Most models carry Studebaker-Garford designations, although a 1906 example exists with no Garford identification of any kind, labeled strictly as a Studebaker. Some sources state that the Model G-10 also is labeled as a Studebaker.

Production
Unknown.

Specifications

Model	Years	Cylinders	CI	Bore x Stroke	Bhp	Wheelbase (in.)	Bodies*
Model A	1903–04	2	unknown	unknown	8	unknown	5 Ptr
Model B	1904	2	unknown	unknown	8	unknown	5 Ptr
Model C	1904	2	215.9	5.0 x 5.5	16	82	5 Ptr
9502	1905	2	215.9	5.0 x 5.5	15	82	5 Ptr
9503	1905	4	212.3	3.88 x 4.5	20	96	5 Ptr, tc
Model E	1906	4	212.3	3.88 x 4.5	20	98	5 Ptr, tc
Model F	1906	4	285.6	4.38 x 4.75	28	104	5 Ptr
Model G	1906	4	280.6	4.13 x 5.25	30	104	5 Ptr
Model H	1907–8/10	4	280.6	4.13 x 5.25	30	104	5 Ptr
Model L	1907	4	285.6	4.38 x 4.75	28	104	5 Ptr
Model M	1910	4	285.6	4.38 x 4.75	28	104	5 Ptr
Model A	1908–09	4	280.6	4.13 x 5.25	30	104	5 Ptr, tc, rb, ld
Model B	1908–09	4	372.1	4.75 x 5.25	40	114	5 Ptr, rb, li, ld, tb, sc
Model C	1909	4	280.6	4.13 x 5.25	30	104	5 Ptr
Model D	1909	4	372.1	4.75 x 5.25	40	117.5	5 Ptr
G-7	1910	4	372.1	4.75 x 5.25	40	117.5	4/5 Ptr, 7 Ptr, li
G-8	1911	4	372.1	4.75 x 5.25	40	117.5	4/5 Ptr, 7 Ptr, li
G-10	1911	4	297.8	4.25 x 5.25	30	116	5 Ptr

*Bodies: P=passengers (preceded by 4/5, 5 or 7); tr=touring; tc=town car; rb=runabout; li=limousine; ld=landaulet; tb=4–passenger tourabout; sc=3–passenger speed car (speedster).

Price History

95+ point condition 1	1982	1987	1990	Return
To 30 hp	$20,000	$22,500	$25,000	2.8%
40 hp	$22,500	$25,000	$30,000	3.7%

Chapter 3

E-M-F 1908-12

	Fun	Investment	Anguish
Open models	7	4	8
Closed models	3	2	8

"Every Morning Fixit," "Eternally Missing Fire," "Easy Mark's Favorite" and "Every Mechanical Failure" were the unbecoming nicknames for Studebaker's sometime-partner E-M-F. What the acronym really stood for was Barney Everitt (a body, top and accessory manufacturer from Detroit), William Metzger (former ace sales manager of Cadillac) and Walter Flanders (Ford's production manager and plant layout expert), who founded their company in Detroit in 1908. Studebaker arranged to receive half of E-M-F's output and, when Metzger and Everitt left after an argument and took the chief

More substantial looking than its rival, the Model T Ford, the E-M-F 30 helped Studebaker become a volume manufacturer. With the help of 1909 models such as this touring, Studebaker finished fourth in the production race for the first time.

engineer with them, Studebaker obtained complete control of E-M-F. It was finally merged into the new Studebaker Corporation in January 1911. The original partners didn't stay angry: Metzger rejoined his colleagues at Detroit's Everitt Company, and in the 1920s the three built the Rickenbacker car.

Until the association with E-M-F, Studebaker had never ranked as a volume manufacturer; on the shoulders of the E-M-F Model 30, it shot to fourth place in calendar 1909 production, behind Ford, Buick and Maxwell, and in 1911 ranked second, with 27,000 units to Ford's 70,000.

The Model 30's rude sobriquets were, however, in order. Early models lacked water pumps and they overheated chronically. This was soon rectified, but the cars also featured a rear-mounted transaxle, which induced quiet running at the expense of weight. To cut weight, E-M-F used a cast-aluminum transaxle housing, but there were vast reliability problems, and the transaxle was dumped with the E-M-F name when Studebaker began to build cars under its own name in 1913.

What To Look For

The E-M-F saw 50,000 units constructed more than its 4½ years of operation, but they are scarce today. The best model is the two-passenger roadster, built for most of the period; the only closed body style was a 1911–12 coupe. Look for clean, restored examples, with some recent touring mileage, and don't attempt a basket case, which is really general advice for all antiques. The Antique Studebaker Club is a fine source of expertise.

Production

E-M-F Model 30

1909	1910	1911	1912
7,960	15,020	26,827	28,032

Identification

Prominent E-M-F script and identification plates on all models.

Specifications

Bodies: Touring (four-door style in 1912), tourabout (1908–09), Demi-Tonneau, roadster and coupe (1911–12).

Engines: L-head four, 226 ci (4.0 x 4.5 in.), 30 hp (ALAM rating 25.6 hp).

Chassis and drivetrain: Ladder chassis, beam axles, with semi-elliptic leaf springs front and full-elliptic rear. Dual ignition (magneto and battery), thermo-syphon cooling retrofitted and later standard with centrifugal water pump. Selective three-speed sliding gear transmission in rear transaxle.

Dimensions: Wheelbase 106 in. (1908–09), 108 in. (1910–11), 112 in. (1912).

Price History
95+ point condition 1
E-M-F Model 30

1982	1987	1990	Return
$18,000	$20,000	$25,000	4.2%

Flanders 1910–12

	Fun	Investment	Anguish
Roadster/runabout	6	5	7
Touring	5	4	7
Closed bodies	4	2	7

The recurring impossible dream of a better Model T convinced Walter Flanders, after Everitt and Metzger had dropped him, to set up shop for himself in Detroit. The result was the Flanders 20, more or less a moonlighting project, since Flanders was running E-M-F for Studebaker at the same time. South Bend, however, certainly approved of the Flanders project.

Trying to undercut Ford, Flanders priced his basic touring body at $750, but this price advantage was soon erased by Henry Ford's ongoing series of price cuts. (The Tin Lizzie runabout went from $825 in 1908 to $590 by 1912.)

Flanders did manage to produce more than 30,000 cars during his brief fling, and the Flanders 20 scored a number of impor-

Handsome and desirable, the Flanders 20 suburban from 1912 represents the highest production year for the marque. These are historic and desirable cars, but unfortunately hard to find.

tant performances. It ran without a stop for repairs in the 1911 Glidden Tour, held the class speed record at Indianapolis, the hill-climb record at Worcester Dead Horse Hill and ran nonstop from Montreal to Mexico City, nearly 11,000 miles. In its final 1912 manifestation the 20 was promoted as a "2 in 1" car—Studebaker dealers selling a touring or roadster with an extra coupe body for the cold months at $1,050 f.o.b. Detroit.

The Flanders was built in the former plant of the Deluxe Motor Company, which Studebaker was convinced to buy for his use by Walter Flanders, and all 20s were sold by Studebaker dealers.

What To Look For

Flanders are interesting cars with a good pedigree, but extremely scarce. The little two-passenger runabout is the most desirable model, but anyone determined to own a Flanders will have to take what's out there, or wait until something shows up.

Production

	1910	1911	1912	1913
Model 20	5,603	9,633	14,562	909

(Fred Fox and Bill Cannon, *Studebaker: The Complete Story*, Tab Books, 1981. Fox and Cannon state that the figures are from an article in the *New York Herald-Tribune*.)

Identification

Flanders script and identification plates.

Specifications

Bodies: Runabout, four-passenger touring, with the addition of a roadster, coupe and suburban (1911–12).

Engines: L-head four, cast en bloc with two main bearings, 169.6 ci (3.63 x 3.75 in.), 21 hp.

Chassis and drivetrain: Ladder chassis with subframe support for motor, steering gear and radiator, rear-mounted transaxle with three-speed sliding gear transmission, beam axles with semi-elliptic leaf springs front, full-elliptic rear.

Dimensions: Wheelbase 100 in. (1910–11), 102 in. (1912).

Price History
95+ point condition 1
Roadster/runabout

1982	1987	1990	Return
$17,500	$20,000	$22,500	3.2%

Other models

15,000	18,000	20,000	3.7

The suburban sans top and windshield took on a sporty air that complemented its reputation for stamina: Flanders set its class speed record at Indianapolis during 1911.

Chapter 5

Fours and Sixes 1913–19

	Fun	Investment	Anguish
Roadster	6	3	5
Touring	5	2	5
Closed bodies	3	1	5

During the first twelve years of the young century, Studebaker was making its way into the horseless carriage business, trying several different approaches. (Horsedrawn vehicles, remember, remained in production through 1917.) Studebaker also involved itself with various other companies—E-M-F, Flanders, Tincher, Garford and so on—both as suppliers of components and builders of complete cars. By 1912 the various decisions had been made. From 1913 Studebaker would build its own gasoline-powered cars.

The first chief engineer was James G. Heaslet, who engineered the Flanders. Heaslet had set up Studebaker's first engineering

Mr. J.M. "Wheelbarrow Johnny" Studebaker, toward the end of his life in a 1916 Model ED Six touring driven by vice president J.G. Heaslet. This is an historic photo, with Frederick Fish, left, and A.R. Erskine in the back seat.

laboratory in 1911 and hired, among others, Fred Zeder, who went on to become famous at Chrysler as part of the Zeder-Skelton-Breer engineering triumvirate. Upper management, too, was entering a period of change: in 1915 J. M. Studebaker retired as board chairman. He was replaced by his son-in-law Frederick Fish, and Albert Erskine became president of the corporation. Erskine would see the firm reap profits and success through the 1920s, but would die in despair, and by his own hand, over the failures of the 1930s.

The Studebaker Fours of 1913–18 were the standard-bearers, the low (or lowish) priced cars that built Studebaker into one of the nation's leading automobile producers in those years. (Studebaker ran third behind Ford and Willys-Overland in 1913–14, but tapered off thereafter as Buick, Dodge and Chevrolet began producing in volume.) These were not cars of the Model T ilk, but they *were* cheap, listing for as little as $875 in 1913; there was always a Studebaker priced under $1,000 in this period.

The dominant body was the touring, which everybody preferred in those days, though there was a handful of sedans, coupes and roadsters. The Sixes were up-market, higher-priced and necessarily of lower production, with more elaborate body styles including seven-passenger limousines.

A 1913 Six seven-passenger touring. Though produced in some quantity, almost 20,000 units, these cars are extremely rare today. Body design of the Four was similar but wheelbases shorter.

What To Look For

Only three Studebaker Sixes from this period are known to exist; one is in a museum, one in Australia.

Some Studebaker collectors say the transaxle is still a weak link on this car, despite the changes made from E-M-F, but with so few around there is a shortage of general knowledge.

There are more Studebaker Fours around than there are Sixes from this period, but we are not talking about vast numbers. Nor is this any place for the money-lined investor: antique Studebakers are going nowhere in terms of appreciation these days, which is no doubt just fine by antique Studebaker collectors, who buy the cars for love not money. The big AA35 Four was a one-year-only model, unfortunately not offered in roadster guise but most commonly built with a touring body. A coupe, which featured "Japanese leather dashboard trim, plate glass and nickel plated controls," would be quite a find.

Identification

Changes were made year by year. 1913: Right-hand drive. 1914: Gas tank in cowl, bead molding on hood, beveled-edge front fenders, gas filler cap on cowl, left-hand drive. 1915: Gas filler cap on right side of instrument panel. 1916: Floor-housed folding jump seats in touring. Fuel tank moved to rear during 1916 production. 1917: Reversible front passenger seat, folding jump seats in touring. 1918: Called Light Four, with low-slung, smoother lines, this was one of three new 1918 models, the others being the Light/Special Six and Big Six; rear door trailing edges slant diagonally upward.

Production

	1913	1914	1915	June 1915–Jan. 1918
S Series (4 cylinder)	15,000	17,976	24,849	80,842 (SF); 8,900–12,500 (SH)
A Series (4 cylinder)	10,000			
E Series (6 cylinder)	3,000	7,625	8,751	60,712

Specifications

Model	Years	Cylinders	CI	Bore x Stroke	Bhp	Wheelbase (in.)	Bodies*
SA25/SC	1913–14	4	192	3.5 x 5.0	25	101	tr, rd
AA35	1913	4	259	4.13 x 5.0	35	115	tr, cp, sed
E6	1913	6	289	3.5 x 5.0	40	121	tr, li
EB/EC-6	1914–15	6	289	3.5 x 5.0	40	121	tr, lan/rd, 2dr sed†
SD	1915	4	192	3.5 x 5.0	30	108	tr, rd
SF	1916–17	4	236	3.88 x 5.0	44	112	rd, lan, 7Ptr, a/w sed
ED	1916–17	6	354	3.88 x 5.0	54	122	7Psed a/w‡
SH	1918–19	4	192	3.5 x 5.0	40	112	rd, 5Ptr, sed

*Bodies: tr=touring, rd=roadster, cp=coupe, sed=sedan, lan=landaulet, li=limousine, 5P=five passenger, 7P=seven passenger, a/w=all-weather.
†EC six offered as five- and seven-passenger touring only in 1915.
‡ED six also offered rd, lan/rd, tr, coupe, sed, li bodies in 1917.

Serial Numbers

1913: 301501–315611 (SA), 101501–110614 (AA); 600001–602800, 602953–603002 (E).
1914: 403001–420515, export 400001–400007 (SC); 605001–612450 (EB).
1915: 423001–447419, export 449001–449443 (SD); 500001–504483, 613001–617155, export 603001–603183 (EC).
1916: 460001–474180, export 449001–449443 (SD); 637261–655270, 200000–207500, export 624001–624865 (ED).
1917: 474181–500369, 100000–109500, export 453229–455926 (SF); 637261–655270, 200000–207500, export 624866–626023 (ED).
1918: 109501–144051, export 10001–12906 (SF); 133101–141975, Canada 12951–up (SH); export 20001–21334 (ED).

Price History

95+ point condition 1	1982	1987	1990	Return
Fours	$12,000	$14,000	$16,000	3.7%
Sixes	12,500	15,000	18,000	4.7

Chapter 6

Special and Light Six 1918–26

	Fun	Investment	Anguish
Roadster	6	3	5
Touring	5	2	5
Closed bodies	3	1	5

Studebaker first called the Special Six the Light Six but, since an even Lighter Six was in prospect, Special Six was the name that stuck. It was light mainly in relation to the Big Six, whose design it duplicated on a somewhat smaller scale. The main engineering difference in the beginning was the Special Six's nondetachable cylinder head; a bolt-on head was used beginning in 1920.

Like the Big Six, the Special Six marked another transition from earlier themes, abandoning the troublesome rear-mounted transaxle for a behind-the-engine transmission, and adopting a humpy rear frame to provide jounce room for the Hotchkiss rear axle. The bodies, too, were thoroughly modernized, with curves replacing corners and smooth lines replacing harder-edged forms that had grown unfashionable.

The Special Six was a canny piece of salesmanship, because it offered Big Six looks with smooth, six-cylinder perfor-

THE STUDEBAKER SPECIAL-SIX 2-PASSENGER ROADSTER

Special Six two-passenger roadster from 1923: a desirable body style from a much improved period. The identifying round cowl lights at lower windshield corners can be seen; teardrop roadster bodies were sleek for the early 1920s.

THE STUDEBAKER LIGHT-SIX 2-PASSENGER COUPE-ROADSTER

The Model EM Light Six of 1923, with the two-passenger coupe-roadster body, duplicated the style of the previous 1923 Special Six, but with closed coachwork. Good performance can be expected from these relatively light cars with their 40 hp engine. Production was more than 118,000, so there are some left around.

mance (a Four was markedly lumpy by comparison in those days) for a much lower price. Touring, roadster, coupe and sedan bodies were offered, including a handsome four-passenger Club Roadster also known as the Chummy. The successor Models EL (with a new dry disc instead of cone clutch) for 1922–24 and EQ (with changes similar to Big Six Model EP) carried on through 1926.

The last of Studebaker's wave of new sixes was the Model EJ/EM Light Six of 1920–24, for which the company spent $15 million to build South Bend's all-new Plant 2. (Plant 1 built components; other Sixes were assembled at Plant 3 in Detroit.) A new design aimed at people ready to graduate from Ford or Chevy four-cylinder motoring, the Light Six rode a 112 in. wheelbase and sold for $1,500–$2,150. Its 207 ci engine had inclined valves and an aluminum head and produced 40 hp.

One Light Six touring continued Studebaker's reputation for record-breaking that had begun with the Flanders 20. Serial number 1004045 was built October 29th, 1920, and shipped to Chester Weaver, a San Francisco dealer, who put it through a series of gruelling tests resulting in several records. It was the first car to enter Yosemite National Park over one of the auto roads in 1921, bucking snowdrifts as high as ten feet; it held the coast route record, San Francisco to Los Angeles, at nine hours, sixteen minutes; and it ran from Los Angeles to Phoenix, mostly over little-marked desert tracks, in thirteen hours, sixteen minutes.

What To Look For

These are handsomely styled cars that deserve more attention and are worth it because they are from a neglected era, the late teens and early twenties. Furthermore, they are overshadowed by the Big Six, and prices have remained modest. The best Special Sixes are the roadsters, both two- and four-seat, the latter Chummy in particular. Open models of the Light Six are equally desirable.

An interesting Special Six from the EQ series was the Sheriff, a touring body carrying the Big Six engine. The EQ series also offers the widest variety of body styles, including Duplex phaetons and roadsters (solid tops, pull-down windows), a Victoria, Brougham, Country Club coupe and coach. Especially handsome among the closed cars is the Berline town limousine for five, handsomely furnished in mohair and wool with silk curtains.

Noisy rear ends are a congenital problem on these cars, but the racket does not seem to disturb the running of the car. They will not cruise as effortlessly on tour as a Big Six, but they are ruggedly built, good-looking and far more capable than the four-cylinder cars in Studebaker's class.

While there's no apparent money to be made with Light and Special Sixes, there's a lot of fun to be had for the dollar; trophy

Production

	1918–19	1920–21	1922–24	1925–26
Special Six	25,801(EH)	68,616(EH)	111,443(EL)	53,780(EQ)
		1920–21	1922	1923–24
Light Six		35,000(EJ)	49,000(EJ)	118,022(EM)

collectors ought to consider them, too, because the typical multiera Studebaker meet rarely includes much competition from like models.

Identification

Special Six: Called Light Six on introduction in 1918; rounded, smoother lines than previous models; rounded roadster rear deck; new four-seat Club Roadster. 1920–21: No change in designation but teardrop-shaped cowl lights adopted. 1922–24: New EL series. Cowl ventilation; larger windshield with large round cowl lights (rectangular on closed cars, teardrop bodies on roadsters) at windshield corners. 1925–26: New EQ series. Drum-style headlamps; Sheriff model adopted.

Specifications

Model	Years	CI	Bore x Stroke	Bhp	Wheelbase (in.)
EH Special Six	1918–19	289	3.5 x 5.0	50	119
EJ Light Six	1920–22	207	3.13 x 4.5	40	112
EH Special Six	1920–21	289	3.5 x 5.0	50	119
EL Special Six	1922–24	289	3.5 x 5.0	50–55	119
EM Light Six	1923–24	207	3.13 x 4.5	40	112
EQ Special Six	1925–26	289	3.5 x 5.0	65	120

Bodies: Special Six: sedan, touring and coupe (1918–24), two-seat and four-seat (Club) roadsters (1918–23), four-door roadster (1918–22); 1925–26 Model EQ: sedan, coach, Duplex phaeton and roadster, Victoria, Berline, Brougham and sport roadster. Light Six: touring, roadster, sedan, coupe roadster (1921–22, 1924), coupe (1923–24), Custom touring (1924).

Dimensions: Wheelbase 119–120 in. (Special Six), 112 in. (Light Six); weight 2,900–3,300 lb. (1918–22 Special Six), 3,065–3,650 lb. (1923–24 Special Six), 3,360–3,890 lb. (1925–26 Special Six), 2,500–2,900 lb. (Light Six).

Serial Numbers

Special Six. 1918–19: 233501–257464, Canada 21351–23256.
1920–21: 257465–290000, 504501–535876, Canada 23257–up.
1922: 3000001–3039122, Canada (including 1923–24) 3050001–3053230.
1923: 3039123–3075316. 1924: 3075317–312000. 1925: 3120001–3161001, Canada (including 1926) 3053231–3054180. 1926: 3161002–3172932.

Price History

95+ point condition 1	1982	1987	1990	Return
Special Six:				
Duplexes & sport roadster	$15,000	$19,000	$20,000	3.7%
Other open models	12,500	15,000	17,500	4.3
1924–25 berline	9,000	11,000	13,000	4.7
Other closed models	9,000	9,000	10,000	1.3
Light Six:				
Open models	11,000	13,000	15,000	4.0
Closed models	8,000	8,000	9,000	1.5

Chapter 7

Big Six 1918–26

	Fun	Investment	Anguish
Roadster	7	6	3
Touring	7	5	3
Closed bodies	4	2	3

The Big Six was Studebaker's postwar flagship—handsome, rugged, high on performance and good-looking in a period not noted for automotive elegance. Its 60 hp, L-head engine departed from previous practice mainly in its detachable cylinder head, but the drivetrain forsook the unit transmission-rear axle in favor of what we now know as conventional, placing the gearbox behind the engine, adopting Hotchkiss drive and linking the two with a Spicer driveshaft.

The initial Model EG Big Six came with only a touring body until 1921, when a sedan

The relatively long, low lines of the Big Six are evident in this photo of the initial 1918 model with touring body. Note the distinctive headlamp treatment, common to 1918–19 models.

and coupe were added. Its successor, the Model EK, had no change in specifications other than a single dry-plate clutch, but gained detail improvements such as a cowl vent, windshield wipers, nickel-plated radiator shell and bumpers, stoplights, motometer and disc wheels during its production run. The succeeding Model EP had somewhat higher compression, full pressure lubrication and a transmission mounted behind the engine, along with more robust engine interior components.

The Big Six really built Studebaker's budding reputation for, as the company itself later termed it, "Style and Stamina." Paul Hoffman's distributorship in Los Angeles (Hoffman would later save the company as president during the 1930s) sold one car that racked up 500,000 miles in little more than five years on the road, mostly for a Los Angeles newspaper distributor; its engine never had to be rebuilt. Another feat was the transcontinental record, which Ab Jenkins and his Big Six Sheriff broke in 1926, crossing from New York to San Francisco in eighty-six hours, twenty minutes. This amounted to a 40.2 mph average, was sixteen hours below the previous record and over six hours shorter than the fastest train time! Studebaker pointed out that with fifty makes on the American market, only seven equaled the Big Six in horsepower, "and they sell for two to four times its price."

Collectors today echo those praises of long ago. One whom I interviewed, a sophisticated collector of many high-class makes, admitted that he prefers his Packards for show, but on tour he'll drive his Big Six Sheriff or President every time: "They cruise effortlessly at 60 mph and handle well with quick, light steering. Packards are trucks by comparison." Maybe that's why so many Packards were chauffeur-driven.

What To Look For

The Big Six's two-wheel mechanical brakes are a fine system for what it is, but they are by no means up to the car's performance. You can easily overdrive the brakes. Studebaker spent $1 million telling the public that four-wheel brakes were dangerous, but in 1925, responding to dealer complaints of sales lost to better-braked competition, the company offered a four-wheel hydraulic system pumping off the transmission for $75 extra, throwing in disc wheels when the system was specified.

Fred Fox and Bill Cannon, in their excellent model history *Studebaker: The Complete Story* (Tab Books), describe the four-wheel system in detail, noting that braking power was greater on the rear wheels than the front. This was purposely designed to pre-

vent front-brake lock, but in doing so, of course, designers lost sight of the main objective: slowing the car. Most collectors say that the four-wheel system was nevertheless far superior to the two-wheel arrangement, but it is so rarely encountered that few are able personally to experience it. Studebaker went to four-wheel mechanical brakes in 1927 and forgot hydraulics for a time.

Big Six speedster, probably 1922, with the optional disk wheels that transform the appearance. Round headlamps with nickel bezels and one-piece windshield marked the physical changes for this year.

THE STUDEBAKER BIG-SIX 4-PASSENGER SPEEDSTER

With nickel-plated radiator shell and disk wheels, the 1923 Big Six looked better than its predecessors, and open models like this speedster are sought after. The 1924 was identical. Big

Sixes like this have all the panache of much more pretentious cars, yet still cost relatively little to own and enjoy.

A 1924 Big Six touring takes on a more modern look with new balloon tires and natural fir artillery wheels. Note the handsome door and passenger-assist handles and the beveled fender edges. This was a beautifully executed car for its day, and its roadability is respected by today's antique car enthusiasts.

A peculiar characteristic of later Big Sixes is that the transmission sometimes locks in second gear, apparently caused by indents in the rod. Another area of concern is the canvas U-joints which easily wear out from lack of maintenance; these should be carefully checked. Starters often need rebuilding, and distributor gears are pot metal, though brass replacements exist.

The Model ER Big Six of 1925–26 was really the perfection of the breed and is the most desirable of this fine Studebaker series today. It will outperform most Classic Car Club of America (CCCA) rated classics, runs smoothly and noiselessly at modern highway speeds; it is a great driver's car.

Identification

Long, 120 in. wheelbase with smooth, curving lines; fourteen louvers on each side of hood; distinctive headlamp housings, oblong with curved sides. 1920: Cowl lights at windshield corners. 1921: Lube fittings replaced oil cups on chassis lube points; reverse curve to rear edge of rear fenders. 1922: New round headlamps with wide nickel bezels, one-piece windshield, left-side exterior courtesy light, cone clutch. 1923: Nickel-plated radiator shell and bumpers; standard windshield wipers, brake lights. 1924: Serial numbers are only distinction from 1923. 1925: Higher compression and horsepower, full-pressure lubrication, transmission and engine in unit and gearbox subframe eliminated, balloon tires standard; optional four-wheel brake system. 1926: serial numbers only distinction.

Specifications

Bodies: Seven-passenger touring (1918–22); coupe (1922–24); seven-passenger sedan (1922–26); speedster (1923–26); seven-passenger Duplex and five-passenger Sport phaetons (1925–26); brougham, berline, club coupe and five-passenger sedan (1925–26).

Engines: L-head six, 353.8 ci (3.88 x 5.00 in.), 60–65 bhp (1918–24), 75 bhp (1925–26).

Production

	1918–19	1920	1921	1922–24	1925–26
Big Six	11,757	14,970	6,277	48,892	147,099

Chassis and drivetrain: Ladder chassis with transmission subframe (1918–24), subframe eliminated (1925–26); selective sliding transmission (1918–24), three-speed manual gearbox (1925–26); semi-elliptical leaf springs all around.

Dimensions: Wheelbase 126 in. (1918–24), 120 in. and 127 in. (1925–26); weight 3,175 lb. (1918–20), 3,300–4,100 lb. (1921–24), 3,500–4,200 lb. (1925–26).

Serial Numbers

1918–19: 290001–301050; 1920–21: 315701–335069; 1922: 2000001–2017139; 1923: 2017040–2027499; 1924: 2027500–2060000; 1925: 2060001–2073000; 1926: 2073001–2102299.

Canada: 1918–19: 29001–30138; 1920–21: 30139+; 1922: 2050001–2050736; 1923: 2050737–2051276; 1924: 2051277–2052200; 1925–26: 2052201–2053099.

Price History

95+ point condition 1	1982	1987	1990	Return
1918–22 touring	$12,500	$15,000	$16,000	3.1%
1923 speedster	14,000	17,500	19,000	3.9
1925–26 phaeton & roadster	16,000	19,000	22,000	4.1
1925–26 Sheriff	13,000	17,000	19,000	4.9
Closed bodies	9,500	10,000	12,000	3.0

Chapter 8

Standard Six and Dictator 1925–37

	Fun	Investment	Anguish
Open bodies	6	7	4
Closed bodies	1	2	4
1932 St. Regis brougham	4	7	4
1934–35 Land Cruiser	6	3	4

The name of the inspired wag who changed the title of Studebaker's mid-range Standard Six to Dictator in 1927 is lost to history, but he or she certainly had a sense of humor, or irony. Dictators were of course more in vogue in 1927. Mussolini made the trains run on time and signed a treaty with the Pope; Hitler hadn't been heard of. Another decade and Studebaker would conclude that the name was more of a liability.

The Model ER Standard Six, introduced in the autumn of 1924 as a 1925 model, was more a prelude to the Dictator than an extension of the Light Six, since its 241.6 ci L-head was considerably larger than the Light Six's and would power all the early Dictator models. To be sure, the 241 was a simple bore job on the Light Six engine, and the Light Six had first brought out full-pressure lubrication. But the Standard of-

The original Model ER Standard Six, first offered as a 1925 model, with the handsome, square-cut berline body for five passengers. Closed Standard Sixes such as this are in relatively good supply, but demand is low. Dictators are scarcer.

Cops meant business in Lincoln Park, Michigan, where South Bend products chased the Detroit variety. This photo nicely illustrates the interesting Duplex top on the two Standard Sixes, a phaeton and roadster. The Duplex was permanently installed and used sliding windows instead of side curtains. Note the Atalanta radiator mascots on both these unmarked cars.

Camping, 1927 style, with a Custom Sedan, probably still called Standard Six rather than Dictator at this time; radiator louver count and other obscure features make exact identification difficult. Note the distinctive and typical double-fluted front bumper and Atalanta mascot.

fered rather better performance than a simple displacement increase would suggest, having higher compression and, initially, twenty-five percent more horsepower.

Of historic importance (and the bane of restorers), Studebaker took the decision, with the Standard Six, to make changes when necessary, rather than annually at new model time. "The worst feature of the yearly model change is the sensational advertising with which [the cars] are exploited," read one Studebaker ad, which has the ring of immediacy today, now that the annual change has been largely discredited. Studebaker was certainly marching to its own drummer with this policy in 1925; but it lasted only while the company was prosperous. By 1931, it was back to model years again. Between 1925 and then, however, it may be misleading to refer to Studebakers simply by model years; model designations would be a lot more accurate.

The downside of the evolution policy was the vast number of running changes, which resulted in Standard Sixes and early Dictators that are decidedly different, although they may share the same model year or have been titled originally in the same year. Fox and Cannon identified the major changes affecting interchangeability in their book, *Studebaker: The Complete Story.*

Though it didn't break records with the regularity of other models like the President, the Dictator did average over 60 mph on twenty-four-hour runs on the Atlantic City, New Jersey, boardtrack in 1927; and the following year a Dictator roadster racked up 5,000 Atlantic City speedway miles at a similar speed. In all, the Dictator broke twenty-eight distance and time records, which was never equaled by a car of its (70 hp) class.

The Dictator continued with the Standard Six's engine and 113 in. wheelbase until

1930, when an Eight was added that was in use through 1932. Several wheelbase and engine shuffles then took place, but power was always a little better as the models evolved. The final Dictators of 1936–37 were the hottest, producing 90 bhp out of 218 ci, about 0.41 bhp per cubic inch, a worthy figure for a Six, especially in those years. Dictator bodies were mostly closed, though a roadster and convertible sedan replaced the previous touring in 1932 and a roadster was offered in 1935.

The Dictator line was scrubbed for 1933 because of the near expiration of Studebaker Corporation, which had been ailing for several years and went into receivership in March. It was reinstated as the bottom-line Six in 1934 and occupied this position for the next three years. Its 1938 replacement was the Commander.

What To Look For

Standard Sixes are in good supply, Dictators less so, especially from around the Depression years. The most desirable cars are of course the open ones, roadsters, phaetons and tourings (in that order) through 1931, the roadster and phaeton (about equal) in 1932 and the 1935 roadster.

Among the semi-closed cars the most desirable, but unfortunately not often seen, are the Duplex phaetons, roadsters and tourings of 1925–27. The Duplex was a patented Studebaker design, a permanent hardtop with novel sliding windows instead of side curtains. The idea was to offer the comforts of a closed car at a lower price—about $400 or $500 below a conventional sedan in those days. This design was a kind of converse to the hardtop convertible of the postwar years, when the object was to offer the openness of a convertible at a lower price. With the advent of all-steel bodies in the thirties, companies were able to offer closed cars at the same or lower price than open ones. The four-door sedan and two-door coach became the dominant styles instead of the old tourings and roadsters.

The Big Six 354 of 1926–28 has a doubtful "ball and ball" two-stage carburetor which was no good new, according to firsthand owner testimony. It idles roughly, returns seven to twelve miles per gallon and is a general nuisance. New replacements are available and should be routinely installed.

The favored year for the Dictator is 1932, the last season for the Dictator Eight. The 1932 model was not common (6,000 were built), but it was a vintage of great beauty. The 1932 was the climax and culmination of the classic Greek revival style, at least as far as Dictators were concerned, since they didn't reappear in 1933. Bodies were sleek, complemented by the handsome new St. Regis brougham with its block-long doors; windshields were cocked at a rakish angle with safety glass all around. There was also a synchromesh freewheeling and optional Startix automatic start. You could order Dictators with chrome-plated wire wheels, and Regal equipment (chrome or painted wires, sidemounts, whitewalls, trunk rack, flying bird hood ornament, chrome-plated horns, armrests on sedans and broughams), and yet pay only $1,200 for a coupe. This would have been considered a bargain in prosperous times, but of course the car market had disappeared by then, and Studebaker nearly went with it.

It must be noted that the odds of finding open Dictators are slight if not nonexistent. The 1932 phaeton and roadster (total production for all 1932 Studebakers was only 26,000) and the 1935 roadster (total production was 44,000) are hardly models you'll find in the stalls at a swap meet. Restoration is warranted whatever their condition; none should be considered a parts car. Collectors who like to drive their cars state that the four-wheel mechanical brakes (1927 on) are preferable to previous arrangements.

Among later (1934–37) Dictators, the open cars are again much sought after, while the scarce but rakish sweptback 1934–35 Land Cruiser four-door sedan remains among the most beautiful Studebakers ever made. There was even a woody wagon in the final 1937 Dictator line, although the bodies were not built by Studebaker and examples are scarce. The 1934 models used an odd and not-much-respected Steeldraulic braking system, mechanical in spite of its name. From 1935, however, reliable hydraulic brakes were standard.

The 1934 Custom Sedan for six passengers, available on Dictator, Commander and President chassis; this example is likely to be a Dictator, judging by the wheelbase. Handsomely styled with elongated rear fenders and radiator at a rakish angle, these bodies were replaced in June 1934 by . . .

. . . the "Year-Ahead" line, deftly restyled, this being the Dictator St. Regis sedan for five passengers in non-Regal trim. The horizontal bonnet louvers gave the Year-Ahead Dictator a still more streamlined and advanced look. Now, try to find one.

A 1937 Suburban, with bodies furnished by outside suppliers, based on the coupe-express chassis. Relative to the mid 1930s the final Dictators, produced this year, were not as distinctively styled.

Production

Standard Six: 1925–26 Series ER 147,099; 1927 Series EU (including Dictator) 65,333.

Dictator: 1928–29 GE 48,339; 1930 GL 17,561; 1931 Series 53 22,371, Series 54 23,917, Series FC (8 cylinder) 16,359, Series 61 (8 cylinder) 14,141; 1932 (8 cylinder) 6,021; 1934 45,851; 1935 "1A" 11,742, "2A" 23,550; 1936 "3A" 26,634, "4A" 22,029; 1937 "5A" 50,001, "6A" 39,001.

Identification

The 1925–26 Model ER: New 241.6 ci engine and 113 in. wheelbase, two-wheel mechanical brakes, single bar bumpers flanking oval bar in center. The 1927 Model EU: "Atalanta" radiator mascot, temperature and gasoline gauges, distinctive double-bar fluted bumpers; mechanical U-joints on late Dictators. The 1928–29 Model GE: Mechanical fuel pump and double-fluted bumpers, rounded radiator shell (first series), smooth double-bar bumpers, rounded radiator shell (second series), windshield visor (third series closed models except club sedan), radiator shell composed of flat section. The 1930 Model GL: Six cylinders, double-drop frame and lower-slung bodies, no emblem on headlamp bar. The 1930 Model FC: Eight cylinders, styling as above, no emblem on headlamp bar until serial 2122868. The 1931 Model 61: Eight cylinders, freewheeling, coupe and sedan only. The 1932 Model 62: Longer 117 in. wheelbase, synchromesh, Startix automatic start systems, safety glass, vee'd front bumper, raked windshield.

The 1934 Model FA: Six cylinders (ex-Rockne engine), front ventipanes, skirted front fenders, angled radiator, bird mascot. For 1935: Narrow grille, hydraulic brakes, downdraft carburetor, radio speaker in headliner over windshield. Solid front axle (Model 1A) or Planar front suspension (2A). For 1936: Die-cast grille sloped at greater angle, longer headlamp pods, straight front bumper, bullet-shaped taillights, optional Hill-Holder; solid front axle (Model 3A) or Planar front suspension (4A). For 1937: One-piece alligator-style hood, rounded radiator with horizontal bars with grille theme repeated at hood sides, rotary door latches. Solid front axle (Model 5A) or Planar front suspension (6A).

Specifications

Model	Years	Cylinders	CI	Bore x Stroke	Bhp	Wheelbase (in.)
ER	1925–26	6	241.6	3.38 x 4.50	50	113
EU	1927	6	241.6	3.38 x 4.50	50	113
GE	1928–29	6	241.6	3.38 x 4.50	67	113
GL	1930	6	221.4	3.38 x 4.13	68	115
FC	1930	8	221.0	3.06 x 3.75	70	115
61	1931	8	221.0	3.06 x 3.75	81	114
62	1932	8	221.0	3.06 x 3.75	85	117
A/AA	1934–35	6	205.3	3.25 x 4.13	88	114
A	1936–37	6	217.8	3.25 x 4.38	90	116

Bodies: Business coupe (1927–28, 1936–37); berline (1927–28); brougham (1930, 1932); cabriolet (1929–30); club sedan (1930–31); coach (1925–26); convertible sedan (1932); coupe (1925–28, 1930–31, 1934–37); Duplex phaeton/roadster (1925–26); Duplex touring (1927–28); landau sedan (1931); Land Cruiser sedan (1934–35); phaeton (1925–26); roadster (1925–28, 1931–32, 1935); sedan (all years); station wagon (1937–on); touring (1927–28, 1930–31); victoria (1927–30).

Serial Numbers

Standard Six: 1202001–1284000 (1925), 1284001–1346100 (1926); 1951351–1954400 (Canada 1925-26); 1346001–1410000, Canada 1954401–1956277 (1927).

Dictator: 1346101–1410000 (1927 EU); 1410001–1437600 (1928 GE), 1437601–1460000 (1929 GE); 1460001–1477300 (1930 GL); 2120001–up (1930 FC); 9000001–9015000 (1931 Model 61); 9015001–9021000 (1932 Model 62); 5145001–up (1934); 5500001–5512000 (1935 Model 1A); 5212001–5235000 (1935 Model 2A); 5512001–5535000, Los Angeles 5850001–5852800 (1936 Model 3A); 5235001–5255000, Los Angeles 5800001–5802500 (1936 Model 4A); 5536001–up, Los Angeles 5852801–up (1937 Model 5A); 5255001–up, Los Angeles 5802501–up (1937 Model 6A).

Canada: 1954401–up (EU), 1956301–up (GE), 1957401–1957668 (GL), 2950101–2950137 (FC), 9950001–up (61), 9950301–up (62), 5954001–up (A freewheeling), 5960001–up (A standard); 5960501–up (1A), 5955001–up (2A), 5960801–up (3A), 5955801–up (4A).

Price History

95+ point condition 1	1982	1987	1990	Return
1925–28 Duplex models	$12,000	$15,000	$17,500	4.8%
1925–28 roadsters	12,000	16,000	18,000	5.2
1925–29 cabriolets, phaetons, tourings	16,000	30,000	32,500	9.3
Coupes/broughams (8 cylinders)	10,000	11,000	12,000	2.3
1932 open models (8 cylinders)	16,000	30,000	37,500	11.2
1934–35 roadsters	15,000	22,500	26,000	7.1
1934–35 Land Cruiser	7,000	8,000	12,000	7.0
Other closed bodies	6,500	8,000	10,000	5.5

Chapter 9

Commander 1927–42

	Fun	Investment	Anguish
Open bodies	7	8	5
Closed bodies	2	3	5
1932 St. Regis brougham	5	8	5
1934–35 Land Cruiser	7	4	5

The Commander name didn't arrive until a few months into production of the 1927 Model EW, itself a downmarket evolution of the Big Six. The name was certainly coined as a match to the President and Dictator. With a hiatus during 1936–37, the Commander stuck and was still around by the time of Studebaker's quiet death in Hamilton, Ontario, in 1966. Like the Dictator, the early Commanders are overshadowed by the mighty President, but in many ways they share that fine Studebaker's attributes, including its Raymond Loewy styling from 1938 onward.

While the President won most of Studebaker's laurels on the board and paved tracks of the late 1920s and early 1930s, the Commander posted numerous feats of endurance in its own right. The greatest of all has to be the astonishing performance at Atlantic City in October 1927. Here three Commanders averaged over 60 mph for no less than 25,000 uninterrupted miles, a feat no production car had hitherto accomplished. Not only was this a record, it was a new category, since the previous enduro mark was 15,000 miles.

Among the Commander's stunts, my personal favorite is Ab Jenkins' assault on Pennsylvania's Uniontown and Negley hills in May 1928. At the latter, he steamed over the crest in a showroom-stock Commander sedan at 60 mph; later he made it at over 30 mph with all the spectators he could load into the car—cargo weight 2,296 lb. A crowd pleaser, Jenkins then pulled a pretty lady out of the admiring multitude and put her behind the wheel, whereupon Mrs. K.A. Bennett became "the first woman to make Negley Hill in high."

It is difficult to imagine how Studebaker would have built such distinctive cars as it began building in 1938 without the Raymond Loewy influence. The French-born designer sent his best men to South Bend and was often there to supervise in person, commuting with outspoken dislike on the Henry Dreyfus-designed New York Central Twentieth Century Limited. (The Pennsylvania, whose streamlined locomotives were

"Sonny Boy" himself, the great Al Jolson, in his 1929 Commander Eight convertible cabriolet, which was painted a distinctive canary yellow. "I'm crazy about cars," *The Studebaker Wheel* quoted Jolson as saying, "especially good cars."

Elegance and distinction at a modest price: the 1930 Commander Eight Regal brougham for five passengers, which ought to prove, if nothing else, that closed models from this vintage deserve some attention too. Note winged radiator mascot.

of his own design, did not stop at South Bend.)

Loewy's designs drew away from the conventional General Motors look, with smooth, bold, rounded fronts and complementing headlamps, taking their shape directly from Pennsylvania's locomotives. His 1940 models were the most graceful cars of the era; by then, all of the companies from Willys-Overland to Ford were trying to copy his style.

Commanders were fine cars, not only carving out numerous track records, but carrying the novel inventions of chief engineer Barney Roos to a broader public than the President could reach: "Planar" independent front suspension, the Hill-Holder, vacuum power brakes, automatic choke, the Celeron spoke cam gear, Hancock rotary door latches, variable ratio steering, all-steel bodies with turret tops. Engines improved dramatically with steel-backed bearings and light alloy pistons. In 1937 the minimum engine durability test at Studebaker was fifty hours at 4000 rpm, fifty hours at 4500 rpm, and 100 hours wide open. This was often unheard of farther north in Detroit....

Commanders are plentiful in most years, but after the Depression hit production plunged. Cars of 1932-33 are in extremely

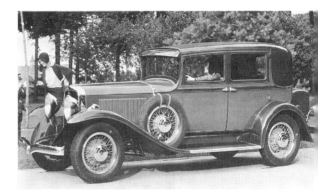

The 1931 Commander Eight Regal brougham for five passengers. Compared to its 1930 predecessor this model wore a single bar vee'd bumper, fender-top parking lights of a distinctively sloped design and no badge bar between the headlamps. Note the application of the trim color around side windows and beltline.

short supply. This is too bad, because these models represented a zenith of the golden age, just before the era of all-steel envelope bodies and art deco streamlining.

What To Look For

Prewar Commanders took a big jump in value during the late 1980s, probably in

35

reaction to major increases for President Eights, some of which obtained Classic status around that time. The open models rose fastest: ten years ago the beautiful 1934–35 Land Cruiser sedan was worth half the price of an early Commander roadster; today the roadster is worth three or more times as much, and the Land Cruiser's value hasn't even kept pace with inflation. This ought to say several things to Studebaker collectors.

The all-weather convertible roadster, a smashing 1933 body style, available on the President and Six as well as Commander chassis. Prominent bird mascot and distinctively sloped radiator and sidelights were notable features.

The four-passenger coupe for 1933, also available on the President and Six chassis; this factory artwork suggests Commander but our opinion is speculative. Skirting had now begun on the front fenders.

The mid 1934 "Year-Ahead" Custom Sedan for six passengers, available on the President and Dictator as well as Commander. Against the run-of-the-mill sedanwork of 1934 this was an elegant closed body style.

The Land Cruiser, whose shape was said to have reflected Phil Wright's brilliant Pierce Silver Arrow, is an exceptional bargain—if you can find one. The open cars have now leveled off and prices are more stable, but relatively soon they'll cost a fortune, and this must be considered.

One closed body style that conversely has soared in value is the lovely St. Regis brougham of 1932; if the value guides can be trusted, it has matched price with several open models. The St. Regis is in a class by itself in terms of style, and is strongly recommended for the serious collector less interested in ninety-three million mile head-room. The 1933 version isn't quite as well proportioned on its shorter wheelbase and sells for a lot less; so do the corresponding sport coupes. But look at those dismal Depression-nadir production figures! The odds of finding these cars being advertised are slim; the best bet is to make friends with "the man who owns one." (Some two-doors were called St. Regis in 1934, but these are conventional coupes and should not be confused with the elegant 1932–33 models.)

Among the later cars, the Loewy-styled 1938–41s are exceptionally handsome in the thirties art deco mode, and the convertible sedan (1938–39) is naturally the preferred

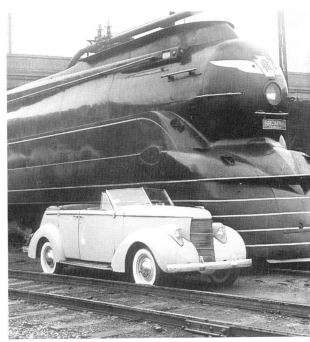

Raymond Loewy's magnificent 1938 State Commander convertible sedan next to its design inspiration—the streamlined head-end motive power of the Pennsylvania Railroad's flagship, the "Broadway Limited." Commander's head-lamps duplicated the knight-like frontispiece of the locomotive. The body style was also available on the President.

Somewhat less impressive a photo, but more useful to restorers, is this factory short of a Commander convertible sedan in plain view; note front fender guides. The President version on a slightly longer wheelbase.

1938 Commander Suburban wagon—with body-work in natural oak, a little-seen body style produced by outside suppliers—appeals to furniture fans but is a very serious restoration project if acquired in less-than-fine condition.

Two-toning shown around the windows is not substantiated in production for the 1940 Commander cruising sedan. This is a heavily retouched and airbrushed photo, possibly for a catalogue.

body style. While the latter isn't cheap, it's a lot less costly than the President version, but examples are few. Among closed body styles, the consensus is that the 1941s are the nicest, with their longer wheelbase, understated divided grille and fender-top parking lamps duplicating the theme of the prow-like hood. The best 1941 is the mid-year sedan-coupe two door, with its then-novel curved, one-piece windshield.

The 1942s received a heavy facelift (by designer Bob Bourke, who later redeemed himself with the 1953 Starliner), which some collectors don't like. They say that it gooked up the lines and aped General Motors. But all 1942s are rare cars and in the Commander's case only 17,000 were built. A mere handful is around today.

A one-piece curved windshield was introduced on Commander and President coupes for 1941. It is partly visible on this Commander Custom sedan-coupe with Deluxe-tone trim. Bulge around wheel radius on rear fenders was a unique feature.

Production

1927: 40,668; 1928: 22,848; 1929–30 Six: 16,019; 1929–30 Eight: 17,527; 1931: 10,823; 1932: 3,551; 1933: 3,841; 1934: 10,315; 1935: 6,085; 1938 7A: 19,260; 1938 8A (State): 22,053; 1939: 43,724; 1940: 34,477; 1941: 41,996; 1942: 17,500.

Identification

For 1927: New EW series based on Big Six but using a substantially shorter wheelbase (120 in.); disc wheels only; teardrop headlamps; double-fluted style bumpers; two-wheel brakes. For the 1928 GB: Four-wheel brakes, mechanical fuel pump, wood spoke wheels standard (wire and disc optional); double smooth bumpers; beltline panel on closed bodies. For the 1928 GH: Mid-year revision featuring longer fenders, winged mascot, headlamp connecting bar with emblem. For 1929–30: Offered with both six (GJ) and eight (FD) cylinders, otherwise virtually identical. Nine-main bearing crankshaft on the eight. Full-pressure lubrication.

For 1931: Eight cylinders only (through 1935). Freewheeling, more horsepower, longer wheelbase; oval headlamps; single bar bumper; no open models. For 1932: Synchromesh gearbox, Houdaille shock absorbers, Startix automatic starter; St. Regis brougham and convertible sedan models appeared. For 1933: Shortest Commander wheelbase to date (117 in.); sloping radiator, downdraft carburetor, automatic choke, Bendix vacuum power brakes.

For 1934: Wheelbase increased 2 in.; round headlamps; St. Regis brougham conventional in design. New Land Cruiser resembled 1933 Pierce Silver Arrow. For 1935: Planar independent front suspension and hydraulic brakes; body styles as in 1934. For 1936–37: No Commanders built.

For 1938: The downmarket Model 7A, at first referred to as a Studebaker Six, was differentiated from the Model 8A Commander, but both models were nearly identical. For this reason the 7A soon became a Commander and the 8A was called State Commander. Visual distinction: conventional pod headlamps for the 7A; Pennsylvania locomotive-style headlamps, beautifully curved and faired into the front fenders, for the 8A. Convertible sedan model returned; optional vacuum gear shift and overdrive with freewheeling. Both models used 116.5 in. wheelbase.

For 1939: Handsome prow-like front end with divided, flanking grillwork; headlamps flush with fenders; steering column gearshift standard (floor shift optional); optional Climatizer fresh air ventilating system. For

1940: Larger windshield, sealed beam headlamps, interior hood locks; open body styles dropped. For 1941: Handsome low-built divided grille, parking lamps in large housing atop fenders; no running boards; longer 119 in. wheelbase. For 1942: Massive one-piece grille encompassing parking lamps with heavy chrome top bar.

Specifications

Model	Years	Cylinder	CI	Bore x Stroke	Bhp	Wheelbase (in.)
EW	1927	6	353.8	3.88 x 5.00	75	120
GB/GH	1928	6	353.8	3.88 x 5.00	85	120/121
GJ	1929–30	6	248.3	3.38 x 4.63	75	120
FD	1929–30	8	250.4	3.06 x 4.25	80	120
70/71	1931–32	8	250.4	3.06 x 4.25	101	124/125
73	1933	8	236.0	3.06 x 4.00	100	117
B	1934	8	221.0	3.06 x 3.75	103	119
1B	1935	8	250.4	3.06 x 4.25	107	119
7A–10A	1938–40	6	226.2	3.31 x 4.38	90	116.5
11A/12A	1941–42	6	226.2	3.31 x 4.38	94	119

Bodies: Business coupe (1927, 1938–39); brougham (1927, 1930–33); cabriolet (1928–30); club express (1938–39); club sedan (1928, 1938–39); convertible sedan (1932–33, 1938–39); coupe (1927–35, 1938–42); Duplex roadster (1927); Land Cruiser sedan (1934–35, 1941–42); phaeton (1927); roadster (1927–30, 1932–35); sedan (all years); two-door sedan-coupe (1941–42); station wagon (1937–on); touring 1929–30; victoria (1927–31).

Serial Numbers

Serial numbers were placed on the left frame rail underfender through mid 1940, left front doorjamb from mid 1940 to 1942. For 1927: 4000001-4039800, Canada 4954401-4955391; 1928 GB: 4039801-4062100, Canada 4955401-4956050; 1928 GH: 4062101-4070500, Canada 4956051-4956214; 1929–30 Six: 40705012-4086041, Canada 4956301-4956904; 1929–30 Eight: 8000000-8025000, Canada 8950001-8950500; 1931: 8025001-8036000, Canada 8950501-8950700; 1932: 8036001-8040000, Canada 8950701-8950800; 1933: 8040001-8043781, Canada 8950801-8951000; 1934: 8045001-up, Canada 8951001-8951200; 1935: 8103000-up, Canada 8951201-up; 1938 7A: 5582001-up, Los Angeles 5857501-up; 1938 8A: 4090001-up, Los Angeles 4800001-up; 1939: 4110001-up, Los Angeles 4802301-up; 1940: 4148501-up, Los Angeles 4807601-up; 1941: 4178801-up, Los Angeles 4811901-up; 1942: 4216501-up, Los Angeles 4816601-up.

Price History

95+ point condition 1	1982	1987	1990	Return
1927–30 open models	$20,000	$30,000	$35,000	7.2%
1928–31 closed models	7,500	10,000	12,500	6.6
1932–33 open models	25,000	40,000	45,000	7.6
1932 St. Regis brougham	13,500	25,000	27,500	9.3
1932 other closed models	10,000	20,000	23,500	11.3
1934–35 open models	15,000	25,000	27,500	7.9
1934–35 Land Cruiser sedan	10,000	11,000	12,500	2.8
1933–42 other closed models	8,000	9,000	12,000	5.2
1938–39 convertible sedan	15,000	28,000	32,500	10.1

Chapter 10

President 1927-42

	Fun	Investment	Anguish
Open bodies	10	10	5
Closed bodies	5	6	5
1932 St. Regis brougham	7	8	5
1934–35 Land Cruiser	7	6	5

The fifteen-year lifespan of the President Eight, in particular the first five years, marked Studebaker's finest hour as a builder of motorcars. The biggest and best Presidents were, as even the Classic Car Club of America (CCCA) now admits, works of art—rolling sculpture. With 300 ci, wheelbases up to 137 in., beautiful but not radical bodywork, they were engineered to a fault. The man responsible was Delmar G. "Barney" Roos, Studebaker's chief engineer from 1927 with experience at Locomobile, Marmon and Pierce-Arrow.

Yet the President was not an expensive car—1928 models started at less than $2,000. At that level it was an unprecedented bargain, and to hear some collectors it's still a bargain today in terms of driving fun and car show admiration. In relative terms, too, it's still underpriced, well below the more famous but less driveable marques of its era.

President bodies of the pre 1934 period had timeless symmetry and cleanliness of line, with a color band at the waistline, crowned and beaded fenders, a chromium-plated radiator shell topped by a Lorado Taft sculpture of the goddess Atalanta. After 1934 they acquired a more rakish beauty, culminating in the brilliant art deco creations of the Raymond Loewy Studios for 1938 and beyond. Anyone who likes cars has to like the mighty President.

The first President was a Six, but it didn't last long. The original Eights were improved by more aristocratic 1929 bodies, achieved through the longer-wheelbase, double-dropped frame, which permitted really striking designs. The 1929s also had more horsepower. The 1931 models grew longer and evolved toward streamlining, with a narrow, vee'd radiator, oval headlamps and neat sidelamps housed in the front fenders. The result was one of Studebaker's all-time styling highlights.

A more streamlined President, one of the first to have benefitted from wind-tunnel testing, was announced in 1933, that grim year when Studebaker almost expired. This Model 92 Speedway offered vacuum-boosted brakes, downdraft carburetors and auto-

Where a lot of collectors would like to be: looking down the 1931 President's long bonnet.

First of the eights, the 1928 seven-passenger sedan featured chrome plating, color panel below beltline, badge bar between headlamps and Atalanta radiator mascot.

Double-drop frame gave lower slung bodies in 1929. This is the Model FE roadster, with Mae West at the wheel, a Studebaker publicity shot. Note the unique pattern of two-toning.

matic heat control for as little as $1,625. That was also the first year for the Model 82 with its smaller engine, the basis of all Presidents to follow for the next ten years.

If the Dictator and Commander had been impressive on the racetrack, the President's record was simply marvelous. The highpoint came at Atlantic City in July 1928, when four completely stock cars drove 30,000 miles in 27,000 consecutive minutes over nineteen days, led by Ab Jenkins of hill-climb fame, Studebaker's perennial champion. By the end of 1928, Jenkins and company held 114 records, thirty-one of which were still standing thirty-five years later.

It was a President that stormed up 14,000 ft. Pikes Peak in a record twenty-two minutes, averaging 34 mph in 1929; and two Presidents that ran away with the class title at the Brooklands Double Twelve (twenty-four-hour) race in England, trailing only the far more powerful Alfa Romeo and Bentley sports cars. President engines powered the Indy racing cars that repeatedly finished in the money at the Indiana classic between 1931 and 1937.

Opinion on the President is remarkably uniform: these are superb road cars, even today. They'll cruise effortlessly at 60 mph on the interstate, handle nimbly on back country roads and respond to steering input with precision that belies the fact that the oldest among them are more than sixty years old. They are to conventional cars of their time as the early Mercer Raceabout was to the cars of the 1910s: overwhelmingly superior over the road.

The higher-geared models may be "a little sleepy on hills," as one owner put it, "but once up to speed it outperforms most CCCA Classics, and it is absolutely noiseless at 55 mph. I have a number of Packards, and for show there's nothing like them—but on a tour I take the President."

What To Look For

Although serious collectors caused Presidents to take a dramatic price leap after the 1929–33 models were declared classics by the CCCA, Studebakers never have and never will be prominent on the auction circuit. They are true hobbyists' cars, and the hobbyists like that situation fine. For this reason it is unlikely that the average prices reported in this chapter will be much disturbed by the odd nutcase who pays a six-figure price for a five-figure car. Presidents were bargains when you could buy a nice roadster for $10,000, and they're still bargains today, whether your purse allows the State Cabriolet or a mere five-passenger

Heavier radiator shell and one-piece dipped-center bumper were characteristics of the 1931s (Model 80 touring shown), along with oval head-lamps and reverse-front sidelamps on fender tops.

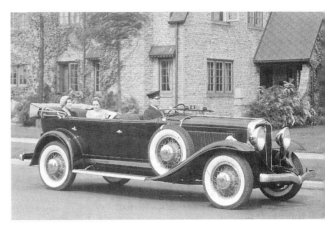

Add whitewalls—this contemporary photo shows rather narrower bands than were usual in those days—and the President becomes majestic. This is a 1931 seven-passenger touring.

sedan. These are fine automobiles, the best not only of South Bend but of the American middle-priced cars of the between-wars period: they will repay the owner with satisfaction both on the road and on the concours circuit.

Much of what collectors favor about President models coincides with what they like about Commanders. The flawless 1932 St. Regis brougham, the dashing Land Cruisers of 1934–35, the art deco Loewy convertible sedans of 1938–39, the posh early limos and sporty roadsters—especially the 1931 Four Seasons convertible roadster—are all high up on the lists. You can tell the relative value collectors place on these cars from the price history.

But there is one important caveat, different from the Commander, and that is scarcity. Production during the early 1930s was infinitesimally small, and in some cases we are speaking academically because not all of the President models Studebaker built are known to exist. The Series 92 is the scarcest of the lot, but all open models of circa 1930 and beyond are in low supply. Since the 1929–33 models are now classics, they naturally command the highest prices; on the other hand they are far and away the greatest among Presidents, with that beautifully built, slow-revving but powerful engine and high standards of fit and finish.

Perhaps the most expensive single model Studebaker today, the 1931 President Four Seasons convertible roadster combines the sturdy Model 90 specification with the most rakish body style. This contemporary photo from an unusual angle shows a full complement of passengers and the rear bumper, which duplicates the front; golf-bag compartment is aft of doors.

Yet, if it's investment you want, consider instead the nonclassic convertible sedans of 1938–39 and (remarkably) the closed cars of 1940–42, particularly the Deluxe-Tone models of 1940–42 and Skyways of 1941–42. These were more luxuriously turned out than the baseline cars: Deluxe-Tones had two-tone interiors with robe rails, assist

43

The 1931 President coupe offered four-seat capacity via rumble seat or two seats only with the underdeck used for cargo.

cords, rear-seat ashtrays, carpeted lower door panels and on sedans, rear ventipanes; the 1941s had a two-tone exterior including a handsome tapered color panel from hood to deck under the beltline. Skyways had chrome bands around the windows, chrome fender lights, two-tone instrument panels, two-tone exteriors and posh, pleated upholstery. The prettiest model of all is the 1941 sedan-coupe, a mid-year introduction, with two doors and a curved one-piece windshield. This model was offered in the Skyway series only for 1941 but in all three President trim variations for 1942.

Production

For the 1927 ES: 9,405; 1928: 13,186; 1929–30: 17,527 (FH), 8,740 (FE); 1931: 6,340 (80), 2,762 (90); 1932: 2,399 (91); 1933: 1,194 (82), 635 (92); 1934: 3,698; 1935: 2,305; 1936: 7,297; 1937: 9,001; 1938: 5,474; 1939: 8,205; 1940: 6,444; 1941: 6,994; 1942: 3,000 (estimated).

Identification

For 1927: Only six-cylinder President. For 1928: New eight-cylinder engine of 313, later 337 ci. Chrome-plated brightwork;

color panel below beltline, Atalanta mascot. Restyled in late 1928 with winged mascot replacing Atalanta; this theme was repeated on the headlamps and sidelamps. FB model has 10 in. shorter wheelbase (121 in.) but same engine. For 1929–30: Double-drop frame and lower bodies; Model FH replaced FB, Model FE replaced FA, with a 10 in. difference in wheelbase (125 in. versus 135 in.). For 1931: Models 80 and 90, with 130 and 136 in. wheelbases, respectively. New, heavier radiator shell and oval headlamps; sidelamps on fender tops; freewheeling; Four Seasons convertible roadster introduced. For 1932: One wheelbase only (135 in.); radiator in wedge shape sloping forward at bottom; winged bird mascot; synchromesh transmission and Startix automatic start standard; St. Regis brougham and convertible sedan introduced.

For 1933: Skirted fenders, more forward slope to lower radiator; Bendix vacuum power brakes, automatic choke, manifold heat control, downdraft carburetor standard. For 1934: New, smaller 250 ci engine; Land Cruiser fastback sedan introduced; parking lights moved off fenders; front

Sleeker than the 1931 President coupe was the 1933 St. Regis brougham, the most desirable closed model from the classic era, also available on the Commander and Six but with shorter wheelbases.

bumper in V shape. For 1935: Planar independent front suspension, overdrive freewheeling standard; radio speaker provision in headliner over windshield; narrow, rounded radiator and flat bumper; grille theme repeated at hood sides; new goddess mascot. For 1936: All-steel tops on closed models; divided windshield with ventilating feature; freewheeling, overdrive, Hill-Holder and Startix optional; grille similar to 1935 but hood side vents narrower.

For 1937: Prominent horizontal grille theme carried on to hood sides; rotary door latches; hypoid rear axle. For 1938: Distinctive new styling with headlamps faired into fenders and matching parking lights outboard; bar grille similar to 1938 but not draped around hood sides; convertible sedan reintroduced. For 1939: Vertical bar grille divided by sharp prow-like bonnet with chrome cap and S monogram emblem; headlamps flush in fenders. For 1940: Similar to 1939 but grille now crosshatched; wide bezels around headlamps which were now sealed beams. For 1941: Divided grille much lower with vertical bars; sedan-coupe with one-piece curved windshield introduced mid-year; Deluxe-tone with color flash on body. For 1942: Full-width grille enclosing parking lamp.

Specifications

Model	Years	Cylinders	CI	Bore x Stroke	Bhp	Wheelbase (in.)
ES	1927	6	353.8	3.88 x 5.00	75	127
FA	1928	8	313.1	3.38 x 4.38	100	131
FA/FB	1928	8	336.7	3.50 x 4.38	109	131/121
FE/FH	1929–30	8	336.7	3.50 x 4.38	115	135/125
90/80	1931	8	336.7	3.50 x 4.38	122	136/130
91/92	1932–33	8	336.7	3.50 x 4.38	122	135
C/1C	1934–35	8	250.4	3.06 x 4.25	110	123
2C/3C	1936–37	8	250.4	3.06 x 4.25	115	125
4C/5C/6C	1938–40	8	250.4	3.06 x 4.25	110	122
7C/8C	1941–42	8	250.4	3.06 x 4.25	117	125/124.5

Bodies: Berline (1928, 1934–35); brougham (1929–33); cabriolet (1929–30); club sedan (1938–42); convertible sedan (1932–33, 1938–39); coupe (1931–37); Duplex phaeton (1927); Land Cruiser sedan (1934–35, 1941–42); limousine (1927–33); roadster (1928–35); sedan (all years); two-door sedan-coupe (1941–42); seven-passenger sedan (1928–29, 1932–33); touring (1928–31); victoria (1928–31).

Serial Numbers

For 1927: 2102301–2119199, Canada 2053101–2053545; 1928 FA: 6000001–6013000, Canada 6950001–6950500; 1928 FB: 7000001–7013500, Canada 7950001–7950200; 1929–30 FE: 6013001–6022000, Canada 6950501–6950700; 1929–30 FH: 7013501–7031000, Canada 7950201–7950500; 1931 90: 6022001–6025000, Canada 6950701–6950800; 1931 80: 7031001–

A 1932 President seven-passenger sedan. A contemporary photo from the Studebaker archives shows the two-tone paint patterns on closed body styles.

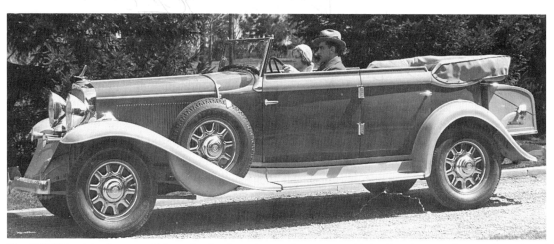

The 1932 President convertible sedan is almost the equal in popularity and value to the Four Seasons convertible, but examples are extremely scarce. Note the two-toning and optional artillery wheels.

7037500, Canada 7950501–7951000; 1932: 6025001–6027400, Canada 6950801–6950850; 1933 92: 6027401–6028017, Canada 6950851–up; 1933 82: 7040001–7041169, Canada 7951001–7951100; 1934: 7045001–up, Canada 7951101–7951200; 1935: 7101001–up, Canada 7951201–up; 1936: 7104001–up, Canada 7951301–up, Los Angeles 7800001–up; 1937: 7111001–up, Los Angeles 7800801–up; 1938: 7120100–up, Los Angeles 7801801–up; 1939: 7125501–up, Los Angeles 7802501–up; 1940: 7133101–up, Los Angeles 7803901–up; 1941: 7139101–up, Los Angeles 7803901–up; 1942: 7145501–up, Los Angeles 7804601–up.

Price History

95+ point condition 1	1982	1987	1990	Return
1927 Duplex phaeton	$17,500	$23,000	$25,000	4.6%
1927–31 touring	22,500	26,000	45,000	9.1
1928–30 other open	25,000	28,000	50,000	9.1
1927–33 limousine	15,000	18,000	22,500	5.2
1927–30 other closed	10,000	12,000	15,000	5.2
1931 80/90 open	28,000	45,000	55,000	8.8
1931 80 sport coupe	14,000	20,000	25,000	7.5
1931 80 closed	12,000	14,000	17,000	4.5
1931–32 90 closed	15,000	18,000	22,500	5.2
1932 St. Regis brougham	18,000	27,000	30,000	6.6
1932–33 convertible sedan	27,000	35,000	55,000	9.3
1938–39 convertible sedan	22,000	30,000	32,500	5.0
1934–35 roadster	20,000	25,000	30,000	5.2
1934–39 closed	10,000	11,000	12,000	2.3
1940–42 all models	7,000	15,000	17,000	11.7

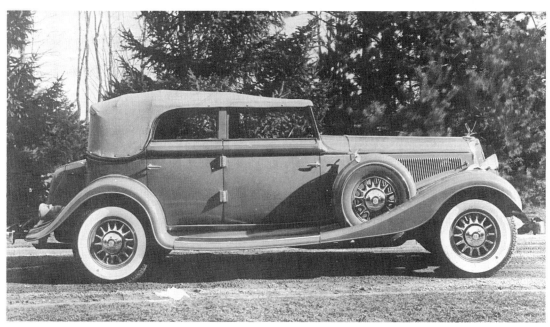

A 1933 Model 92 Speedway President convertible sedan. An interesting comparison to the previous photo, showing the evolutionary skirted fenders and more rakishly angled radiator.

A 1934 President custom sedan for six passengers. This is the early 1934 version, with vertical side hood louvers, which were superseded by the horizontal louvers of the "Year-Ahead" line in June 1934.

Brilliant in concept with its dashing lines, Loewy's fabulous President Land Cruiser of 1935 took as its inspiration Phil Wright's famous Pierce Silver Arrow. It is encouraging to realize that these Land Cruisers are still quite affordable today although availability is slight. They represent the production sedan in one of its highest prewar stages of design development.

A 1935 President Eight six-passenger custom sedan displays the evolving styling, with thin horizontal bar side grilles flowing back from the narrow vertical radiator grille and a goddess serving as mascot. Nicely balanced for a 1935 sedan.

At a wide angle, a contemporary camera catches the swoopy deck of a President five-passenger coupe at a 1937 auto show. Coupes are the closed cars to look for among the later Presidents, commanding a ten to twenty percent lead in value against the less graceful four-door sedans.

In the Pennsylvania locomotive image, the 1938 President State cruising sedan, with its novel headlamps built into the front fenders. If you can't afford a convertible sedan, this four door offers the same styling hallmarks for much less investment. Bodies are exceptionally well built and tight.

49

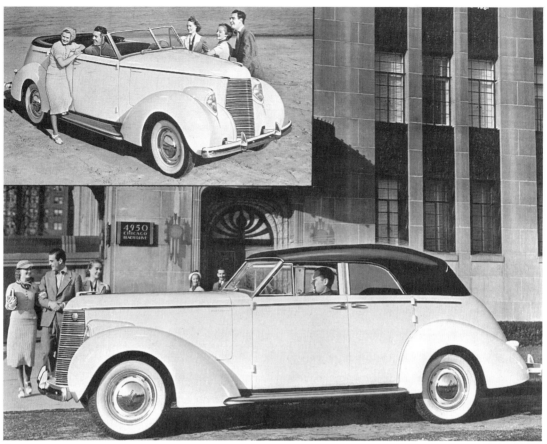

Convertible sedan Presidents of 1938–39 are the most desirable open Studebakers of the late 1930s and now command formidable prices, although they are extremely scarce. No 1939s are known to exist and only one or two 1938s have surfaced.

A 1940 President cruising sedan for export, from the factory archives. The 1940 models comprised the last President until 1955; the 1940 and 1941 are the cleanest.

The 1941 Skyway President Land Cruiser, a desirable closed model, few of which exist. Prewar styling was at its best on the 1941, with its low grille and handsome fender-top parking lamps. A big, quiet, comfortable and luxurious car, this President is ideal for long-haul tours.

The heavy 1942 facelift by Bob Bourke is apparent on this Skyway sedan-coupe for five passengers. This is another airbrushed photo of an earlier model. Note the one-piece curved windshield, first offered on 1941 coupes, a great innovation.

Chapter 11

Erskine and Six 1927–33

	Fun	Investment	Anguish
1931–32 roadster	6	7	7
Other open models	5	5	7
Closed models	2	1	4

On paper, the Erskine was an ideal product. One of the loveliest small cars, it was designed by none other than Ray Dietrich, founder of LeBaron and Dietrich, Inc. To its good looks Studebaker applied a lively Continental-built six, and the sales department offered a wide selection of body styles. But the Erskine failed: largely on the basis of price. As former Studebaker engineer Otto Klausmeyer remembered, in 1927, when the Erskine tourer sold for $945, Ford announced the new Model A at $525. That pretty much says it all.

The project was further hampered by the fact that it initially received only lukewarm promotion in the United States. Its *raison d'être*, Albert Erskine said, was the European market, where small, luxurious sixes were all the rage during his visit in 1924. Alas, the export market proved illusory, because the small six fetish was short-lived, and the Erskine had taken three years to gestate.

Too pricey for the Americans, prematurely obsolete in Europe, the Erskine furthermore carried a mechanical liability. To deal with European horsepower taxes, which were largely based on bore, it had a low-torque "stroker" engine. To compensate and give it some power, Studebaker fitted a fairly low axle ratio of 5.13:1, and this translated into premature engine failure from over-revving.

The Erskine in its first form, 1927; here is the Custom sedan for five passengers.

The Erskine 1927 tourer. Ray Dietrich's touch is evident in the duotone panels at the beltline. Hood ornaments (squatting boy on the tourer and winged god on sedan) do not appear to be stock. Note E hubcaps.

For 1928 the Erskine adopted conventional, double-bar bumpers front and rear and less angular, more conventional lines. Here is the cabriolet.

Studebaker tried to cope by replacing the stroker engine with a larger and squarer six in 1930 and, since the Erskine name had no panache, renamed it the Studebaker Six partway through that year. But management never indulged in the price-cutting that would have been the car's only salvation, probably because that would have meant losing large bags of money on every sale. The Erskine and Studebaker Six sold consistently at the 20,000 unit level through 1932, but by then its continued high price in the teeth of the Depression finished it off, and sales tapered to a trickle.

By that time Studebaker was facing bankruptcy, avoiding this doomsday scenario by entering receivership in 1933. Its namesake remained on as president, but by summer found himself personally bankrupt and in despair. Albert Erskine died by his own hand on the morning of July 1, 1933.

What To Look For

The Erskine has become recognized of late as the little aristocrat that its makers said it was, and values took off in the mid 1980s, especially for open models. Production was low, however, and the cars are scarce. The

The 1928 Erskine five-passenger sedan.

best place to look for them is through club publications and at club meets.

Despite a more personal history than the succeeding Six, the Erskine doesn't seem to command higher prices. Indeed the most valuable of all models is the Six convertible roadster. This is partly due to the roadster's traditional top-rung position among body styles, but also to the fact that collectors prefer the more streamlined 1931–32 Six to the rather angular Erskine sport roadster of 1928.

53

The 1930 Erskine Royal sedan, Model 53, represents the last year for the Erskine brand name. This is a good model year to look for, since it comes with the new Studebaker-built six with more low-end torque. In prime condition a sedan like this may still be available at under five figures.

Open models that should be sought are the rare 1932–33 convertible sedans, in regular or Regal trim. In 1932 Studebaker built a St. Regis brougham on the Six chassis, and this is an especially desirable closed model.

Chances are that you'll not be able to do much picking and choosing of body styles, because survivors are few, highly cherished and rarely traded. My own feeling is that the open Erskines are underpriced and well worth the investment; they certainly make the other small cars of that period, like Hudson's Essex and Nash's Ajax, look like the crackerboxes they are.

One positive quality of the Erskine is its origins as a coachbuilder's product: not *coachbuilt*, of course, for it was manifestly a production car, and an assembled one at that. But in style and stance it was a cut above the conventional 1920s production-line stuff. The late Ray Dietrich said that he always had a fondness for his work on the Erskine, but that it had looked "too European" for contemporary Americans.

Buyers of pre 1930 models should pay particular attention to the engine; what was true of the little stroker in 1929 is still true today. This is not a car for vintage touring at the pace most of those people like to go.

Identification

For 1927: Nerf-style bumpers front and rear. For 1928: Conventional full-width double bumpers, more skirting to fender edges. For 1929: Closer family resemblance to senior Studebakers; 2 in. longer wheelbase; cowl lights behind hood; headlamp bar emblem. For 1930: Studebaker engine replaced Continental stroker; midseason name change from Erskine (E hub emblems and Erskine badge) to Studebaker Six (S hub emblems and Studebaker badge) occurred at serial number 5085001—some badges have migrated back and forth, however. For 1931: Close family resemblance to Commander, with smooth double-bar front bumper dipping to shallow V in center; freewheeling standard; round headlamps (not oval as on

Production

1927	1928	1929	1930	1931	1932	1933
24,893	22,275	25,565	22,371	23,917	13,647	6,861

(Production in 1930 consisted of about 12,000 Erskines and 10,000 Sixes.)

senior models). For 1932: Single bar front bumper (still dipped in center); raked windshield, bird mascot, Startix and safety glass standard; St. Regis brougham model; parking lamps on fender tops. For 1933: Down-draft carburetor, automatic choke, vacuum power brakes; more rakish, streamlined styling with wedgy grille and partly skirted fenders.

Specifications

Model	Years	CI	Bore x Stroke	Bhp	Wheelbase (in.)
Erskine-50	1927	146.1	2.63 x 4.50	40	107
Erskine-51	1928	160.4	2.75 x 4.50	43	107
Erskine-52	1929	160.4	2.75 x 4.50	43	109
Erskine/Six-53	1930	205.3	3.25 x 4.13	70	114
Six-54	1931	205.3	3.25 x 4.13	70	114
Six-55	1932	230.2	3.25 x 4.63	80	117
Six-56	1933	230.2	3.25 x 4.63	85	117

Bodies: Brougham (1930 Six, 1932-33); business coupe (1927, 1930 Erskine, 1931); two-passenger cabriolet (1929); four-passenger cabriolet (1929); club coupe (1927); club sedan (1928-31); convertible roadster (1928, 1930-33); convertible sedan (1932-33); coupe (1930-33); landau sedan (1930 Six, 1931); sedan (1927-28, 1930-33); touring (1927, 1930-31).

Serial Numbers

For 1927: 5000000-5025000, Canada 5950001-5950250; 1928: 5025001-5047400; 1929: 5047401-5073000, Canada 5950251-5951410; 1930: 5073001-5096000, Canada 5951500-5952000; 1931: 5096001-5120000, Canada 5952200-up; 1932: 5120001-5133400, Canada 5953301-up; 1933: 5133401-5140252, Canada 5953741-up.

A 1933 Studebaker Six all-weather convertible sedan. The Six replaced Erskine in 1930, and 1933 was its last year. The body style was also available on Presidents and Commanders. This is its most junior form, but not many were built, since total Six production was just 6,861 units, the majority with closed bodies.

Price History

95+ point condition 1	1982	1987	1990	Return
1927-28 open bodies	$12,500	$20,000	$27,500	10.4%
1931-32 roadster	15,000	32,000	37,500	12.1
1930-33 other open bodies	15,000	25,000	30,000	9.1
1932 St. Regis brougham	9,000	10,000	12,500	4.2
1927-33 other closed bodies	7,000	9,000	10,000	4.6

Chapter 12

Rockne 1932–33

	Fun	Investment	Anguish
Open models	5	4	6
Closed models	1	1	4

Studebaker refused to give up on small cars, despite the Erskine's failure, and in 1932 launched the only car named for a football coach, Notre Dame's immortal Knute Rockne, who had no sooner given the car his blessing than he died in a plane crash. South Bend was Notre Dame country, and Rockne had served Studebaker for three years in promotional capacities. The tragic death of Rockne seemed almost to jinx the car, but a jinx wasn't necessary, really—the Depression was enough.

Studebaker did not repeat its Erskine errors: it brought the Rockne in at a rock-bottom $585 for the Model 65 coupe and equipped all models with reliable, Studebaker-built engines; the Rockne 75 got the Six's 230. Perhaps the choice of a Detroit factory

ROCKNE PHOTO

The most desirable Rocknes are the open models, but there aren't many Rocknes at all and one like this 1932 Model 65 Deluxe convertible roadster would be quite a find. Note the Flying R bonnet mascot and R monogram on hubcaps. Second color accents appeared on beltline and inboard of running boards.

was a bit odd, but Studebaker had space there, the old E-M-F works, and it wasn't all that far from South Bend. George Graham, late of Willys-Overland, was named vice president of sales, and predicted a new, value-oriented car for people who were fed up with Depression sparcity and wanted more bang for the buck.

Unfortunately this was not quite the case: the doldrums had arrived and people wanted the cheapest wheels they could buy. Ford's Model A undercut the Rockne by $150.

The Rockne 75, initially built in South Bend to get some sample stock, would have replaced the Studebaker Six had it succeeded. It was approximately the same size and used the same engine. The smaller Rockne 65 was a purpose-designed economy car, and despite its short life it gave one long-lived item to Studebaker: its 190 ci six would remain in production for nearly thirty years.

Rocknes were quite elaborately equipped, with all the mechanical contrivances common to senior Studebakers, and such up-market features as adjustable steering column, cowl vents, windshield wipers and airplane-style instruments. Sedans had robe rails, armrests and footrests and interior domelights. For 1933 the line was trimmed

to the 65, rechristened the Model 10, with a slightly longer and lower body. After the receivers took over in the spring of 1933, they initially planned to move Rockne production to South Bend, and the Detroit plant was duly cleaned out. But by mid-year management decided to phase out the Rockne and pin their hopes on a new, broader line of Studebakers. This proved a wise decision as Studebaker clearly had the established name. The Rockne was replaced by a revived Dictator in 1934.

The 1932 Rockne Six Model 65 sedan in an early factory photograph. Again, the novel color accents are visible. Sedan prices do not run with open cars and probably the best sedan you could buy would cost less than five figures.

Factory artwork of the 1932 Rockne Six 75 five-passenger sedan, which rode a 4 in. longer wheelbase and used a slightly larger six with more horsepower.

The V-motif on the radiator was an identifying trait of most Rocknes. This 1933 Deluxe shows the altered front fenders, which were redesigned to conceal the chassis underneath, and twin chrome-plated horns, which were standard equipment.

What To Look For

The Rockne 75 convertible sedan and roadster are handsome cars, as good as anything in the class of 1932—but you hardly see any. The few Rocknes around tend to be the conventional closed jobs that comprised the bulk of production. If a Rockne comes your way it should be topless; if not, it should at least be painted in bright colors. I remember photographing a Model 10 coach—twenty years later I can still recall its handsome paint combination: light and dark blue and cream. I am not at all sure that paint job was authentic, but it sure made an ordinary car interesting.

Production

Sources differ, some stating 23,201 for the entire period, others 22,715 for 1932 and 13,326 for 1933.

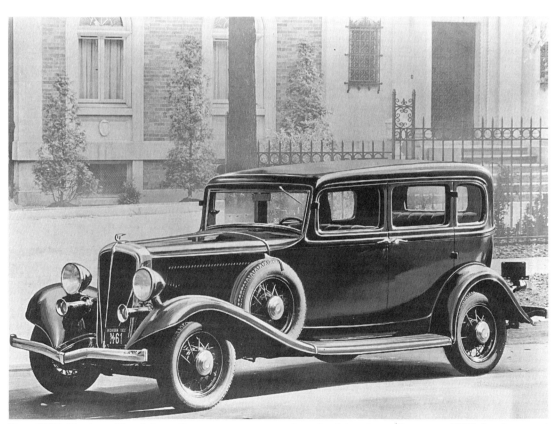

The 1933 Rockne Six deluxe five-passenger sedan, probably originally a 1932 model but air-brushed to show the new 1933 fenders and standard horns.

The 1933 Rockne Six deluxe convertible sedan, probably the most desirable model but rarely if ever seen. Studebaker was advertising "room for five, a top that is raised or lowered with ease, and a 70–horsepower motor that gives surprising performance." Price guides quote figures of more than $30,000 for this model in prime condition but the price is speculative because there are no established sales. It is likely that such a Rockne would be exchanged quietly between private parties.

Identification

For 1932: Rockne badges, prominent V motif in radiator grille; single bar bumper dipped in center; 18 in. wheels; Model 65 has sloping hood louvers, Model 75 vertical louvers. Deluxe trims versions are identified by flying R stylized radiator mascots. For 1933: Safety glass windshields; slightly longer and lower bodies; 17 in. wheels.

Specifications

Bodies: Two- and four-passenger coupe, sedan, roadster, convertible sedan; five-passenger coach (1933).

Engines: L-head six, 205.3 ci (3.25 x 4.13 in.), 72 bhp (1932 75), 189.8 ci (3.13 x 4.13 in.), 66 bhp (1932 65), 70 bhp (1933).

Chassis and drivetrain: Ladder chassis, three-speed synchromesh transmission, freewheeling standard.

Dimensions: Wheelbase 110 in. (65, 10), 114 in. (75); weight 2,495–2,645 lb. (65 and 10), 2,825–3,000 lb. (75).

Serial Numbers

For 1932 65: 00001–16150, Canada 960001–960750; 1932 75: 1500001–1507400, Canada 1960001–up; 1933: 16151–29386, Canada 960751–961299.

Price History

95+ point condition 1	1982	1987	1990	Return
65 roadster	$20,000	$25,000	$33,000	6.6%
65 convertible sedan	18,000	25,000	30,000	6.6
75 open models	20,000	25,000	32,500	6.3

Chapter 13

Champion 1939–46

		Fun	Investment	Anguish
Champion		3	1	2

Writers are used to heaping plenty of blame on Harold Vance and Paul Hoffman for the postwar decisions that contributed to Studebaker's decline. Putting ourselves in their shoes *at the time*, however, would we have made wiser choices? Who knows? Besides, Vance and Hoffman need to be remembered for their positive accomplishments: like saving the company from a wipeout in the mid 1930s, and for assuring it a fresh start with the 1939 Champion.

Hoffman in Sales and Vance in Production moved fast to save the firm in 1933. Pierce-Arrow, which Studebaker had acquired in balmier days, was sold at a loss, but it netted

The 1939 Champion three-passenger coupe, least expensive of the Champions, which rewrote Studebaker history and made the company prosperous again after some bleak years. These good-looking little Studebakers are readily available in fine condition for little outlay.

badly needed cash. The production line was restarted after a month's inaction; by 1934 a $7 million line of credit had magically appeared, and a year after that the Los Angeles assembly plant opened. Sales jumped again. Then, in 1939, the Champion put Studebaker over the top.

Lithe-looking with its clean Loewy styling, 600 lb. lighter than the Ford-Chevy-Plymouth trio and therefore lively and economical, the Champion could not have been better targeted for the recovering economy of 1939. Its modern, high-revving L-head six, designed by Barney Roos' replacement, W.S. James, was lightweight but large enough to allow displacement increases for greater power: by 1946 it was producing 80 hp on only 6.5:1 compression. In a 6,000 mile double crossing of the country in 1939, an overdrive Champion averaged over twenty-seven miles per gallon at an average speed of more than 40 mph. Yet at Indianapolis, where the same car was run 15,000 miles at 62 mph, it returned close to twenty miles per gallon. This was quite a little car.

Champions began with three closed-body styles and two levels of trim, and by 1941, when a record 85,000 were sold, there were no fewer than a dozen choices of trims and models. Production in 1942 was truncated, and a little-altered line called Skyway Champions was revived in 1946. These were soon replaced by the all-new 1947 models, however, and less than 20,000 1946s were built.

What To Look For

The best choice among the early cars are the coupes, of course; while the 1940 is richer-looking than the 1939, the 1939 is the historic first. From 1940, look for the two-toned interior and exterior Delux-Tone (Deluxstyle in 1942) models, which also have, as standard, robe rails, carpeted power door panels, rear ventipanes, assist cords, and so on. Midrange Custom models have twin wipers, horns and taillamps, front-door armrests, bumper guards and deluxe steer-ing wheel. The 1941 Delux-Tones also carry two-toned tapering color panel below belt-line. Only one (Skyway) trim state was available in 1946; no two-toned 1946s have been encountered in the field, although air-brushed two-tones appear in some factory photos. Get the best car you can possibly find. Champions will cost far more to re-store than you can ever recover anytime soon; a car in top original condition would be ideal.

Production

1939	1940	1941	1942	1946
33,905	66,264	84,910	29,678	19,275

(1946: Cruising sedan 10,525, club sedan 5,000, three-passenger coupe 2,465, five-passenger coupe 1,285.)

The handsome 1941 Champion sedan looked elegant in dark colors. This was probably the best year for styling among the late prewar cars.

Champions like this are not uncommon and not expensive to acquire.

Airbrushed photo shows a 1942 Champion Custom club sedan, probably altered from a 1941 photo by changes to the grille, which was much heavier than the previous year.

The 1946 Skyway Champion coupe for three passengers saw only 2,465 copies built and is therefore scarce; the five-passenger verison had production of only 1,285. Parking lights rode the tops of front fenders as a distinguishing mark of the 1946s.

Identification

For 1939: Prow-like Loewy front end with flush headlamps; grille composed of central section with bold horizontal bars and flanking sections with thin vertical bars. For 1940: Center grille section composed of more and thinner horizontal bars; sealed-beam headlamps. For 1941: Lower, flatter, vertical bar divided grille. For 1942: Single horizontal bar grille with heavy top frame. For 1946: Upper grille molding extended under headlamps, side hood molding eliminated, nameplate on hood side, wide brightwork added along rocker panel and bottoms of fenders; parking lights on fender tops.

Specifications

Bodies: Three-passenger coupe, club sedan, four-door sedan (1939–42, 1946); five-passenger coupe (1940–42, 1946).

Engines: L-head six, 164.3 ci (3.00 x 3.88), 78 bhp (1939–40); 169.6 ci (3.00 x 4.00), 80 bhp (1941–46).

Chassis and drivetrain: Planar front suspension with transverse leaf spring, live rear axle with semi-elliptic leaf springs, double-acting shocks, three-speed manual gearbox, overdrive and freewheeling optional. Planar suspension adopted safety links and extra leaf in transverse spring (1941).

Dimensions: Length 189–193 in., wheelbase 110 in., weight from 2,260 lb. (1939 Custom three-passenger coupe) to 2,566 lb. (1946 Cruising sedan).

Champion cruising sedan for 1939 is less appealing to collectors and should be passed over if you can get a coupe. There were no open Champions in the prewar years.

Serial Numbers

For 1939: G0001–G30500, Los Angeles G800000–G803700; 1940: G30501–G90100, Los Angeles G803701–G811200; 1941: G90101–G165500, Los Angeles G811201–G821000; 1942: G165501–G192583, Los Angeles G821001–G823645; 1946: G193001–G212279, Los Angeles no production.

Price History

95+ point condition 1	1982	1987	1990	Return
1939–40 all models	$6,000	$7,000	$7,500	2.8%
1941–42 all models	5,000	6,500	8,000	6.1
1946 all models	4,500	5,500	7,000	5.7

Chapter 14

Commander 1947–52

	Fun	Investment	Anguish
Convertible	7	6	4
Coupe (Starlight 1949–52)	6	5	3
Sedans, two door and four door	2	2	3
Coupe, three passenger	3	2	3
Starliner hardtop, 1952	6	5	3

The essential lines of the advanced 1947 Studebakers were conceived by the Raymond Loewy Studios, South Bend's styling consultants, during and just after World War II. Loewy's team was initially headed by Virgil Exner, who was replaced by Bob Bourke after Exner left before the final designs were locked up. Exner, who set up his own freelance design business in competition with Loewy, was actually responsible for the final

details of the car through the aid of engineering vice president Roy Cole, who purposely misled the Loewy people by giving Bourke incorrect dimensions. Livid, Raymond Loewy vowed a comeback, wresting the design responsibility from Exner with the bullet nose 1950 and 1951 models.

Anything as unabashedly new and different as these rakish cars is bound to excite controversy, and there were mainly two

The Commander, on its longer wheelbase, was a better-proportioned car than the contemporary Champion. The last sixes were built in 1950; the convertible of 1949 is shown.

The 1950 convertible can easily be distinguished from the 1951 bullet noses by the heavy chrome moldings surrounding the nose and the head- lamps and parking lamps. Only 2,867 of this model were built.

Here is the 1951 version of the same convertible body style. The bullet nose was toned down and V-8 power was under the hood. The V-8s now lead the sixes slightly in value. Production rose to 3,770.

schools of opinion: you loved it, or you hated it like poison. In retrospect, styling authorities tend to agree that Loewy's men and Exner had created a pioneer design, one that prefigured most competitive styling to follow. Granted, Kaiser-Frazer beat Studebak-

Studebaker paced the Indy 500 in 1952 with a Commander convertible, the last ragtop until 1960. The V-8 convertibles of 1951 and 1952 have increased dramatically in price over the past three or four years, surpassing every other Studebaker in the early postwar period. But 1952s are scarce, with a run of only 1,715 units for the model year.

er into production with the first straight-through fenderline; but Kaiser-Frazer's cars were slab-sided, lacking the interesting surface development of the Studebakers.

The Commander was powered by a hefty six through 1950, and by Studebaker's reliable and powerful small-block V-8 from 1951. The Commander's wheelbase was 7 in. longer than the Champion's through 1950, the difference being ahead of the cowl. With superior trim inside and out, it was clearly the upper-class model, priced about $400 more than comparable Champions, a span equal to about $2,500 in today's dollars.

Commanders are solidly built, fun to drive and not overly complex to restore, though it is easy to spend more on a restoration than the total value of the car. The convertible naturally leads in popularity, but production was small. Stick overdrive was optional throughout this period, while a Borg-Warner automatic gearbox was available from mid–1950.

What To Look For

Regal Deluxe trim, comprising stainless steel windshield borders, seat bases and rocker panel moldings, is desirable. Convert-

A 1952 Commander Starliner hardtop convertible, which could carry five passengers.

ibles came in this form as standard. In 1951 the Deluxe designation was dropped and the standard model became simply the Regal, while the better version, with standard fender ornaments, was called the State model. The V–8 engine is rather more desirable than the six, but choosing a V–8 automatically means you're in for the bullet nose (1951) or shovel nose (1952), and purists think the 1947–49 styling is better. On the other hand, the bullet nose at least has a certain period charm to it, and so resembles the fabled Tucker that some Studebakers were used as Tucker replicas in the race and crash scenes of the recent Tucker movie.

Note that the wheelbase difference between the Commander and the Champion was all cowl-forward; the bodies are no different, so there's no difference in interior space. The Hill-Holder, a pioneering Studebaker option designed to hold manual cars in place on hills, is a worthwhile accessory to look for. The one-piece curved windshield, an advanced idea, was introduced on the convertibles in 1947 and became available line-wide in 1951. The V–8 convertibles, which were once worth less than early sixes, have recently taken the lead, making them the best models if investment is your chief concern.

Identification

For 1947: Body-colored molding on front edge of hood. Parking lights in grille opening form rectangular lamps; Commander in script on left-hand side of hood and Studebaker on right. For 1948: Heavy horizontal chrome upper molding replaced body-colored molding on front edge of hood. For 1949: Stroke increased; model nameplate in script on left side of hood. For 1950: Bullet nose with wide chrome surround; model designation on either side of front fenders. For 1951: Bullet nose surround now body color; one-piece windshield on all models; V–8 engine. For 1952: Longer and lower hood, sloping down to wraparound grille. Studebaker V-shaped crest above grille molding; push-button starter on automatic-equipped models.

Production

	1947	1948	1949	1950
Regal Deluxe:				
Convertible	1,503	7,982	1,702	2,867
Coupe, five passenger	10,557	11,528	6,278	7,375
Business coupe	1,046	1	0	0
Sedan, two door	2,159	1,661	934	2,363
Sedan, four door	13,539	15,685	10,005	14,832
Deluxe:				
Coupe, five passenger	2,742	2,913	2,712	4,383
Business coupe	301	0	0	0
Sedan, two door	548	1,440	1,418	4,588
Sedan, four door	3,485	8,898	6,280	11,440

	1951	1952
State:		
Convertible	3,770	1,715
Starliner hardtop	0	14,548
Starlight coupe, five passenger	11,637	3,784
Sedan, two door	3,903	1,529
Sedan, four door	21,134	9,998
Regal:		
Starlight coupe, five passenger	8,192	5,127
Business coupe	1	0
Sedan, two door	8,034	5,995
Sedan, four door	29,603	22,037

Specifications

Bodies: Two- and four-door sedans, business coupe, five-passenger hardtop (1952 Starliner), five-passenger five-window coupe (Starlight from 1949).

Engines: L-head six, 226.2 ci (3.31 x 4.38 in.), 94 bhp (1947–48); 245.6 ci (3.31 x 4.75 in.), 100 bhp (1949); 102 bhp (1950). Ohv V-8, 232.6 ci (3.38 x 3.25 in.), 120 bhp (1951–52).

Chassis and drivetrain: Three-speed manual, overdrive optional, Borg-Warner automatic optional from mid 1949. Independent front suspension with coil springs and tubular shocks; live rear axle with semi-elliptic leaf springs.

Dimensions: Length 198–208 in., wheelbase 119 in. (1947–48), 120 in. (1949–50), 115 in. (1951–52), weight 3,095–3,375 lb.

Serial Numbers

For 1947: 4232501–4287000, West Coast 4818501–4820500; 1948: 4287001–4360743, Los Angeles 4820501–483598; 1949: 4361001–4398473, Los Angeles 4832701–4838950; 1950: 4398601–4461853, Los Angeles 4839001–4848311; 1951: 8110001–8216497, Los Angeles 8800001–8815942; 1952: 8217001–8289877, Los Angeles 8816001–8826703. (Includes Land Cruisers.)

Price History

95+ point condition 1	1982	1987	1990	Return
1947–49 convertible	$ 9,500	$15,000	$16,500	7.1%
1950 convertible	12,000	17,000	18,500	5.6
1951–52 convertible	10,000	18,000	19,000	8.4
Coupe, five passenger	5,300	5,800	8,500	6.1
1952 Starliner hardtop	5,000	5,500	9,000	7.6
Sedans and business coupes	4,000	5,000	7,000	7.2

Chapter 15

Champion 1947–52

	Fun	Investment	Anguish
Convertible	6	5	4
Coupe (Starlight 1949–52)	5	4	3
Sedans, two door and four door	1	1	3
Business coupe, three passenger	2	1	3
Starliner hardtop, 1952	5	4	3

Studebaker's breadwinner in the early postwar years evolved from the winning-formula Champion of 1939 and remained true to its forebear's purpose: economy transportation for people who didn't like the "low-priced three." Studebaker had a high-overhead plant and Champions were more expensive than comparable Fords, Chevys and Plymouths, but in the car-starved early postwar years people couldn't get enough of them. The Champion had stolen a styling leap on the competition by abandoning its prewar body after 1946 and producing the first low-priced, all-postwar body style two years before the Big Three competition. The little six that powered these cars was a stroker evolution of the original Champion, no great shakes in the performance department but reliable and easy on gas. Champions rode shorter wheelbases than Commanders, but the difference was entirely in the extra 7 in. of front fender ahead of the cowl, so buyers gained no extra passenger or trunk space by opting for the Commander versions. Champions tended to outsell Commanders by about two to one, but in

Little Champion convertibles are enjoying high prices despite their fairly plebian origins. Production of the 1947 model was the lowest after 1952, at only 2,251 units. The one-piece curved windshield was a pioneering feature, exclusive to convertibles in this model year.

Champions were all identical from the cowl forward, but differences were profound among various closed bodes such as this three-passenger coupe and four-door sedan (1948 models; note grille changes). These two cars also illustrate

trim differences: the Regal Deluxe sedan has stainless steel windshield borders and rocker panel moldings, which are missing from the Deluxe coupe. Collectors would still prefer the coupe with its sleeker styling and long deck.

Convertible Champions came only as Regal Deluxes and saw record production in 1948 when nearly 10,000 were built.

Raymond Loewy Studios created the novel Starlight coupe, a historically important car which set new standards of glasswork, and a car now strongly sought after by Studebaker collectors. This is a 1949 Champion Regal Deluxe five passenger.

1950 when Studebaker built more than 300,000 cars and was eighth in model-year production, the ratio was almost four to one.

What To Look For

No engine changes occurred during this period, with the exception of a boost of 5 hp between 1949 and 1950. Automatic transmission was available from 1950, but stick shifts are recommended to take advantage of what little power there is. Styling followed that of the Commander. Construction quality was good throughout, but Champions tended to be harder-used, and not too many mint originals are around. Not a car for the investor and speculator; con-

versely, a nice, inexpensive way to get into the old Studebaker field, and priced so low relative to more desirable Studebakers that you can and should buy the finest example you can find.

On a 112 in. wheelbase, the 1947–49 convertible was the smallest ragtop on the American market in those years, an interesting fact for collectors who like tiny cars. The price-leader 1950–52 Customs (coded W1, F1 or Q1 in the body number) are bare-bones models; try to find a Regal Deluxe instead.

Production

Regal Deluxe:	1947	1948	1949
Convertible	2,251	9,996	7,035
Coupe, five passenger	9,061	8,982	9,828
Business coupe	3,379	823	718
Sedan, two door	12,697	9,471	5,618
Sedan, four door	30,000	30,494	24,328
Deluxe:			
Coupe, five passenger	7,670	5,499	5,917
Business coupe	5,221	3,783	1,642
Sedan, two door	10,860	10,203	10,359
Sedan, four door	23,958	21,436	20,134

	1950	1951	1952
Regal:			
Convertible	9,362	4,742	1,575
Starliner hardtop	0	0	12,119
Starlight coupe, five passenger	29,966	14,103	6,183
Business coupe	849	373	0
Sedan, two door	21,976	8,931	5,534
Sedan, four door	55,296	35,200	20,566
Other models:			
Custom Starlight coupe	3,583	2,781	1,096
Deluxe Starlight coupe	19,028	9,444	6,075
Custom business coupe	1,562	2,429	0
Deluxe business coupe	2,082	961	0
Custom sedan, two door	19,593	10,689	4,310
Deluxe sedan, two door	45,280	18,591	12,989
Custom sedan, four door	16,000	9,972	6,400
Deluxe sedan, four door	46,027	26,019	24,542

Identification

Same as Commander; see preceding chapter.

Specifications

Bodies: Two- and four-door sedans, business coupe, five-passenger hardtop (1952 Starliner), five-passenger five-window coupe (Starlight from 1949).

Engine: L-head six, 169.6 ci (3.00 x 4.00 in.), 80 bhp (1947–49), 85 bhp (1950–52).

Chassis and drivetrain: Three-speed manual, overdrive optional, Borg-Warner automatic optional from mid-1949. Independent front suspension with coil springs and tubular shocks; live rear axle with semi-elliptic leaf springs.

Dimensions: Length 190–198 in., wheelbase 112 in. (1947–49), 113 in. (1950), 115 in. (1951–52), weight 2,585–2,890 lb.

Serial Numbers

For 1947: G212501–up, G824001–up (Los Angeles); 1948: G314501–up, G827301–up (Los Angeles), G700001–up (Canada); 1949: G400501–up, G839701–up (Los Angeles), G703101–up (Canada); 1950: G468101–up, G851801–up (Los Angeles), G709401–up (Canada); 1951: G1000001–up, G889101–up (Los Angeles), G724501–up (Canada); 1952: G1115501–up, G907301–up (Los Angeles), G735701–up (Canada).

Price History

95+ point condition 1	1982	1987	1990	Return
Convertible	$9,000	$13,000	$15,500	7.0%
Coupe, five passenger (Starlight)	4,500	6,000	7,500	6.6
1952 Starliner hardtop	5,000	6,500	9,500	8.4
Sedans and business coupes	4,000	5,000	6,500	6.3

The 1950 Champion Regal Deluxe convertible. Note wheelbase differences from contemporary Commanders, which was entirely ahead of the cowl; the passenger compartments were identical though dashboards differed.

Suicide door configuration of 1947–52 sedans is shown in this 1950 Champion, identifiable by its prominent bullet nose and broad chrome collar. Bumpers were to have followed front-end contour but production economies prevented this from occurring.

A narrower chrome collar around the bullet nose distinguished the 1951 Champion, which is considerably scarcer than the previous model. Champion convertibles in the best show condition command as much as $15,000 today but are a shade cheaper than the Commander versions, especially the V–8 Commanders.

The 1952 Regal Deluxe Champion two-door sedan showed Studebaker's extensive facelift, with longer, lower hood and integrated, wraparound taillights.

Chapter 16

Land Cruiser 1947–52

	Fun	Investment	Anguish
Land Cruiser	4	4	3

Technically the Land Cruiser was a Commander, but Studebaker often tried to sell it as a separate model, and by many measurements it was. A stretched version of the four-door Commander W body, it had its own Y-body designation and its own price tag, $100 or so higher than the Commander Regals. Its most important selling point was its commodious interior, achieved by a truly monumental (for a Studebaker) wheelbase: 123–124 in. through 1950. It shrank slightly after that. In essence, the Land Cruiser was to the Commander what Cadillac's Sixty Special was to the Sixty-two: more of what you liked about the standard model.

The Land Cruiser remained part of the Studebaker line until 1955, when it was superseded by a revived President. It carved out a profitable market niche, with sales remaining brisk until Studebaker as a whole hit the skids in 1953. Incidentally, the 1952 Studebaker sedans were the last with suicide

The Land Cruiser was an extended-wheelbase Commander, built from 1947–52; the 1949 model is shown.

rear doors. Since the Land Cruiser's rear doors were 4 in. wider than the others, watching one of them blow open at speed must have been scary.

What to Look For
Performance came in with the 1951 V-8 engine, and the bullet nose arrived on the 1950 model.

Production
For 1947: 20,519; 1948: 35,731; 1949: 14,390; 1950: 24,712; 1951: 38,055; 1952: 20,117.

Identification
Four-door sedan body only; wing vents in rear doors; longer-than-usual wheelbase, wider rear doors. For model year differences see Commander chapter.

Specifications
Body: Four-door sedan only.

Engine: L-head six, 226.2 ci (3.31 x 4.38 in.), 94 bhp (1947–48); 245.6 ci (3.31 x 4.75 in.), 100 bhp (1949); 102 bhp (1950). Ohv V-8, 232.6 ci (3.38 x 3.25 in.), 120 bhp (1951–52).

Chassis and drivetrain: Three-speed manual, overdrive optional, Borg-Warner automatic optional from mid 1949. Independent front suspension with coil springs and tubular shocks; live rear axle with semi-elliptic leaf springs.

Dimensions: Length 208.5 in. (1947–48), 212 in. (1949–50), 201.5 in. (1951–52); wheelbase 123 in. (1947–49), 124 in. (1950), 119 in. (1951–52); weight 3,155–3,365 lb.

Serial Numbers
Part of Commander series; body number designation Y5 for all years.

Price History

95+ point condition 1	1982	1987	1990	Return
All years	$5,000	$6,750	$7,500	5.2%

Note: Some price guides show Land Cruisers actually slipping in value between 1987 and 1990. This must be caused by erroneous information, since the trend has been steadily upward, albeit gradual.

Most dramatic was the 1950 Land Cruiser with its prominent pointed nose and heavy chrome headlamp bezels—the archetypal six-cylinder Cruiser, although hard to find.

Chapter 17

Starliner and Starlight 1953–54

	Fun	Investment	Anguish
1953 Starliner hardtop	6	6	7
1953 Starlight coupe	7	5	6
1954 Starliner hardtop	6	6	4
1954 Starlight coupe	7	5	3

No mass-production car today is the product of any individual designer, however gifted; nor has there been such a car for a long time. "Why doesn't it look like the prototype?" is a question we've asked of everything from the Mercedes-Benz 190 and BMW M1 to the Pontiac Fiero and Cadillac Eldorado. Of course, Robert E. Bourke's magnificent 1953–54 Studebaker coupes were affected by the same forces present today—engineers, salespeople, upper management. And those people did a degree of damage to his concept. Bean counters pinched pennies on door latches to produce fly-open doors; refusal to make a fifty-cent body alteration produced instant-rust front fenders; a conservative sales executive demanded dull, mouse-grey and dung-brown interiors (though there were trim options to get around some of this); production planners turned out hordes of sedans when they should have at least kept the flow of coupes going, and both models demanded more quality control than they got. But none of this affected the skin-deep elegance of what has come to be accepted as the finest single American automotive design of the 1950s— and one of the best this century.

As head of Raymond Loewy's styling department at South Bend, Bourke was left

An early 1953 Commander Starliner, showing the tri-star hood emblem, which was protested by Daimler-Benz. Purists hold the 1953 a better design than the 1954 for its cleaner grille, but from a mechanical and quality standpoint the 1954 was the better car. Champion versions shared the same body but had six-cylinder power and S logos instead of V–8 emblems.

mainly alone by Loewy, a brilliant judge of talent who knew whom he had working for him. Since Loewy got the blame when sales went wrong, he fully deserved the popular designation of the Starliner and Starlight as "Loewy coupes."

Assisted by Holden Koto, Bourke sculpted a fuselage inspired by the Lockheed Constellation airliner, the tail cut on an angle almost identical to the Connie's. Resisting every effort by chrome-conscious managers (and Loewy on occasion) to gook up the car with bright metal, Bourke specified a simple divided grille, no chrome at all along the body sides, a vast glass area, a relatively flat roof, a hood and deck free of tinsel. Salespersons demanded a hood ornament, but it remained an option.

The details were as good as the overall shape: modest bumpers faired beautifully into the bodywork; taillights that were elegant in their simplicity; an avant-garde "S-in-circle" identifying logo, with the obligatory nameplates worked unobtrusively into the grille bars. (Mercedes protested the 1953 model's early star emblem, which was accordingly scrubbed.) Withal, the Starliner and Starlight were classic pieces of design, which swam against the tide, proving that not everybody in America built ugly dinosaurs, even in darkest 1953.

While Studebaker's public reacted favorably to the coupes, the factory inevitably expected to sell a lot more sedan models, which had been dummied up by Bourke to mimic the coupe lines on a shorter wheelbase. The production ratio was close to four sedans per coupe, but buyer demand was almost the opposite, swelled by people who had never looked at a Studebaker until they saw the 1953 Starliner. Hasty shifts in the model mix and the rush to get them into production prevented the production of quality jobs, and the factory's high overhead precluded a competitive price. Bourke estimated that the same car could have been built by General Motors to sell for $300–400 less than Studebaker's list price of $1,955–2,502.

What To Look For

Acquiring a Loewy coupe is largely a matter of opportunity. A fairly good supply exists, but they're not often advertised and many sales occur quietly among friends.

It is of crucial importance that your purchase is rust-free, whatever the model. These cars rust with abandon, and the damage is often structural, requiring heroic restoration efforts. On the other hand, body parts are obtainable, and you can't say that for most thirty-five-year-old cars.

Dramatically beautiful, Bob Bourke's Starliners are considered by many as the outstanding American automotive design of the 1950s. This is the 1954 Commander version, with V-8 emblems to remind viewers of its 232 ci power plant and egg-crate grille to differentiate it from the 1953 model.

While the Starliner hardtop with its pillar-less construction is the connoisseur's choice, the Starlight coupe is a much more solid affair and priced considerably cheaper, car for car in the same condition. Deciding which body style you want is something you should do before you go shopping. Starliners leak, rattle and flex; Starlights are relatively tight. The latter came in two trim states: Deluxe (pretty plain stuff with the aforementioned mousy interiors) and Regal (considerably upgraded).

Another curious trade-off: the style of dashboard depends on the engine fitted, or vice versa. If you buy a Champion, you get the underpowered L-head six and a conventional dash with the instruments grouped under an oblong glass cover; if you buy a Commander, you get the sprightly overhead-valve V-8, but the instruments are housed in binnacles, with hoods that look like a row of traffic lights, down around your knees where you won't have to look at them. I favor the Champion dash and the Commander engine.

All-vinyl pleated upholstery is a desirable option. It can add up to twenty-five percent to a car's value compared to standard cloth and vinyl upholstery in a car of similar condition.

Avoid cars that have been foolishly gooked-up by accessory-happy restorers: hood ornaments, gas-flap edge guards, jumbo rearview mirrors, foglights and extra bumper guards ham up this fine design. If they're present, get rid of them.

Production

	Starliner	Starlight
1953 Champion	13,058	25,488
1953 Commander	19,326	20,858
1954 Champion	4,302	12,167
1954 Commander	5,040	6,019

Identification

Single horizontal grille bar (1953) or egg-crate grillwork (1954); Champions carry "S-in-circle" logo and Champion grille script; Commanders carry V8 logo and Commander grille script.

Specifications

Bodies: Five-passenger hardtop (Starliner), five-passenger five-window coupe (Starlight).

Engines: L-head six, 169.6 ci (3.00 x 4.00 in.), 85 bhp (Champion); ohv V-8, 232.6 ci (3.38 x 3.25 in.), 120 bhp (Commander).

Chassis and drivetrain: Three-speed manual, overdrive optional, Borg-Warner automatic optional. Independent front suspension with coil springs and tubular shocks; live rear axle with semi-elliptic leaf springs.

Dimensions: Length 202 in., wheelbase 120.5 in., weight 2,700–2,825 lb. (Champion), 3,040–3,175 lb. (Commander).

Serial Numbers

Contained within overall Champion and Commander serial number spans (see next chapter). Body style designations (within body numbers): K5 for Starliner hardtop, C5 for Regal Starlight coupe, C3 for Regal Deluxe coupe.

Price History
95+ point condition 1

	1982	1987	1990	Return
Champion Starlight	$3,500	$5,500	$ 7,500	10.0%
Champion Starliner	4,000	6,500	8,500	9.9
Commander Starlight	5,000	6,000	9,500	8.4
Commander Starliner	5,500	7,000	10,000	7.8

Note: Although the 1954 is much scarcer, prices are roughly equal year to year because the 1953 is the first and the purer design—despite its dreadful brakes.

Chapter 18

Sedans and Station Wagons 1953–58

	Fun	Investment	Anguish
Sedans, 1953–58	1	1	3
Station Wagons, 1954–58	2	2	3

Circumstances required Studebaker to put up with the same basic sedan and wagon bodyshells from 1953 until the advent of the Lark in 1959—and even the Lark was a derivation of the original Bob Bourke pillared sedan shell of 1953. Circumstances are stubborn things. This company had been mismanaged with a vengeance since World War II, granting everything a powerful union demanded while rival manufacturers were negotiating compromises and taking strikes. Asked in Senate antitrust hearings during 1958 whether he didn't think the Big Three had put the independents out of business, General Motors chairman Frederick

Donner replied: "And when did you stop beating your wife? If you are thinking of Studebaker-Packard, did you ever stop to wonder what they did with the profits of the lush war years? If they reinvested them in the business? We didn't drive them to their present condition. They drove themselves there." (Studebaker finally took the inevitable strike in January 1955, at the peak of the mid-decade boom, losing thirty-six precious days at exactly the wrong time. As usual, its timing was flawless.)

Quite frankly these are some of the ugliest and most boring cars of the 1950s, and there is not much praise for them. The best

Best choices among sedans of this period are early vintages and luxury models, such as the 1954 Land Cruiser. Chrome rub-rail was plastered over bodyside sculpture at the behest of the sales department, which wanted more glitz. Sedans are cheap, $5,000 being enough to buy one of the best examples.

In mid 1955, bodies were altered. Here is the original body, shown on the Champion Regal, with an unwrapped windshield.

The new Ultraview windshield on the President State was the chief component of what Studebaker called Ultra Vista styling. The President also displayed optional gimcrackery such as foglights and bumper guards, fendertop ornaments, rear fender skirts.

were probably the 1954s, which had the benefit of all the quick fixes the factory did to correct the ill-assembled 1953s, plus the still unsullied lines of Bob Bourke. (Bob Bourke is one of the few designers who admits he goofed with a design; try and find

a designer who will confess to having had something to do with the Edsel, for example.)

For 1955 the Loewy team had to hang on gobs of chrome and an ugly wraparound windshield. Vince Gardner then became responsible for the 1956–57 facelift, Duncan McRae for the 1958 with its grotesque quad headlamps and tack-on tailfins. (Dunc, too, admitted what he had wrought, but rightly pointed to the 1958 absurdities the rest of the manufacturers were building.)

Lacking quads and tailfins, but even uglier in its plainness was the stripped Scotsman, by which Studebaker attempted to compete with the Big Three, pricing the cheapest model at $1,776 against about $1,885 for the baseline Chevy. A $100 difference was a lot in 1957—but not enough to convince Americans to forsake a successful maker with a high resale record for a Scotsman.

The problem really wasn't the Bourke-Gardner-McRae styling, which was quite in keeping with mid 1950s norms, but with the rapidly aging bodyshell, which was simply too high and narrow to apply itself properly to the longer, lower and wider 1950s idiom—and Studebaker (by 1956 allied by shotgun wedding to Packard) was unable to afford a new shell.

What To Look For

For connoisseurs of styling (however ironic that may be in this particular field), the 1954 Conestoga wagon is the class of the bunch. The only models that really fit Bourke's original styling were the original cars, the 1953s and 1954s. Studebaker did not offer a Conestoga in 1953, so the 1954 is the sole choice, available either as a six or as a V–8, the latter being more desirable.

In 1955 Studebaker revived the President, on the longer hardtop wheelbase, offering two versions of four-door sedan plus coupes and hardtops. The following year, however, only the President Classic was on the long wheelbase, a replacement in kind of the old Land Cruiser, which had breathed its last in 1954. At the same time all hardtops became Hawks, but Presidents still came in two versions of four door, a two door and a wagon. The 1958 President line was whittled to a solitary (long wheelbase) sedan and the novel Starlight hardtop.

The cars look best in the most elaborate models, though, so a President is a better choice than a Champion (six) or Commander (eight). Presidents also came with hotter V–8s than Commanders.

Ironically, the model from this group that has appreciated most strongly over the past eight years is the plain-Jane Scotsman. A fetish for these truly stripped cars has developed, or perhaps they're so ugly folks can't help but feel sorry for them. But restorers have been seeking them out. The cost of restoration is probably several thousand dollars less than for a President. Although some of the basic materials that went into Scotsman interiors are nonexistent nowadays, there's no chrome plating to speak of, and that costs the world.

Another minor flurry of interest has developed over the 1954 Conestoga wagon, a car with fairly low production numbers and no 1953 counterpart. It is the only model other than the Scotsman from this group that has appreciated in value by a rate greater than ten percent per year since 1982.

Studebaker's continuing and increasing sales problems during 1955–58 resulted in some extremely uncommon permutations, even among the standard listed models, not to mention a handful of experimental variants. If rarity is important to you, some of the figures at the end of the production charts will blow your mind.

Production

	1953	1954	1955
Champion:			
Custom four door	5,496	2,860	3,290
Custom two door	3,983	2,653	2,801
Deluxe four door	17,180	9,668	13,621
Deluxe two door	7,564	4,449	7,666
Deluxe Conestoga two-door wagon		3,910	3,517
Regal four door	17,897	7,286	7,406
Regal two door	2,968	1,066	
Regal Conestoga two-door wagon		3,074	1,372
Commander:			
Custom four door			2,082
Custom two door			1,413
Deluxe four door	10,065	4,615	16,768
Deluxe two door	2,371	1,086	6,834
Deluxe Conestoga two-door wagon		1,912	4,280
Regal four door	7,454	2,571	9,985
Regal Conestoga two-door wagon		2,878	2,516
Land Cruiser	15,981	6,383	
President:			
Deluxe four door			1,021
State four door			14,634

Production

Champion:	1956	1957	1958
Custom four door (1958 Econ-O-Miler)	1,170	2,106	1,118
Custom two door		1,751	
Deluxe four door	11,983	8,313	5,178
Deluxe two door	4,301	1,950	1,455
Deluxe two-door sedanet	3,097		
Regal four door	1,180	247	
Pelham two-door wagon	2,236	3,400	
Commander:			
Custom four door	335	828	
Custom two door		530	
Deluxe four door	14,700	10,285	6,771
Deluxe two door	3,663	2,077	
Deluxe two-door sedanet	1,523		
Parkview two-door wagon	3,333	738	
Provincial four-door wagon		3,995	2,412
President:			
Four door	6,822	3,127	
Two door	1,914	836	
Four door 120 in. wheelbase (1956–57 Classic)	8,507	6,063	3,570
Pinehurst two-door wagon	1,522		
Broadmoor four-door wagon		1,530	
Scotsman:			
Four door		3,005	7,654
Two door		2,943	5,538
Two-door wagon			7,680

Note: In addition to these regular models, the *Standard Catalog of American Cars 1946–1975* reports the following scarce, probably trial, variations: 1957 Champion two-door wagons 26; President four doors: 74 Custom and 33 Deluxe; President two doors: 62 Custom and 8 Deluxe; President wagons: 8 Deluxe two doors and 6 Custom four doors. 1958 Champion Deluxe wagons 12; Scotsman V–8 wagons 7, two doors 44 and four doors 37; Scotsman "Marshal" (President V–8-powered police model) wagons 70, two doors 152, four doors 115; President Deluxe four-door wagons 1.

Identification

For 1953: Divided grille with horizontal bars, Champion or Commander script on bars. For 1954: Divided grille has egg-crate mesh instead of bars. For 1955: Grille formed by oblong opening with modified V insert; large square parking lights under headlamps and switch key starting. Custom: no trim around front and rear windows; Deluxe: chrome trim around front and rear windows; Regal and President: as Deluxe plus chrome trim around side windows, President with script identification. President State: chrome molding length of body and chrome fender trim above headlamps. For 1956: Egg-crate grille not full width and not wrapped at sides; Commander and President with V-8 engines; President with chrome panel between wheel wells. Cyclops eye speedometer on sedans and wagons. For 1957: Full width wraparound grille with dual headlamps; Scotsman stripped of all bright-work and script identification. Custom: belt molding ends behind center post; Deluxe: full-length belt molding; Commander: as Deluxe with V-8 engine; President: two-piece belt molding on fender, usually two-toned inside. For 1958: Grille similar to 1957 but Studebaker in block letters replaces emblem on hood.

Specifications

Bodies: Four- and two-door sedans and wagons.

Engines: L-head six, 169.6 ci (3.00 x 4.00 in.), 85 bhp (1953–54 Champion); 185.6 ci (3.00 x 4.38 in.), 101 bhp (1955–58 Champion and Scotsman).

Ohv V–8, 232.6 ci (3.38 x 3.25 in.), 120 bhp (1953–54 Commander and Land Cruiser); 224.3 ci (3.56 x 2.81 in.), 140 bhp (early 1955 Commander); 259.2 ci (3.56 x 3.25 in.), 162 bhp (later 1955 Commander), 170 bhp (1956 Commander), 175 bhp (1955 President), 180 bhp (1957 Commander), 185 bhp (late 1955 President, optional 1956 Commander, standard 1958 Commander), 195 bhp (1957 Commander). Ohv V–8, 289.0 ci (3.56 x 3.63 in.), 210 bhp (1956–57 President), 225 bhp (optional 1956 President, standard 1957–58 President).

Chassis and drivetrain: Three-speed manual, overdrive optional, Borg-Warner automatic optional. Independent front suspension with coil springs and tubular shocks; live rear axle with semi-elliptic leaf springs.

Dimensions: Length 202–206 in., wheelbase 116.5 in., 120.5 in. on 1955 and 1958 President and 1956–57 President Classic, weight 2,680 lb. (two-door Scotsman) to 3,420 lb. (President Broadmoor wagon).

Serial Numbers

Champion: 1953: G1197501–G1270324, California G917701–G927156; 1954: G1274001–G1315831, California G927401–G932286; 1955: G1316501-up, California G932501-up; 1956 (including Flight Hawk): G1357501–G1379117; 1957 (including six-cylinder Silver hawk): G1379201–G1405239, Canada G769101–G772216; 1958 (including Scotsman and six-cylinder Silver Hawk): G1405401-up, Canada G772301-up.

Scotsman: 1957: 1399130-up. 1958: included with Champion.

Commander: 1953: 8290001–8353332, California 8826801–8836505; 1954: 8354901–8380448, California 8836801–8841029; 1955: 8380601-up, California 8841201-up; 1956 (including Power Hawk): 8429601–8454060, California 8849101–8852866; 1957: 8454101–8471491, Canada 8962601–8965076; 1958: 8471601-up, Canada 8965101-up.

President: 1955: 7150001-up, California 7805001-up; 1956 (including Sky Hawk): 7171001–7188817, California 7808501–7811699; 1957 (including V–8 Silver Hawk): 7188901–8209836, Canada 7901501–7901916; 1958 (including V–8 Silver Hawk): 7210001-up, Canada 7902001-up.

Stylist Vince Gardner worked on a shoestring budget to modernize the 1956 line; here was his new President Classic sedan. Note two-tone pattern around window frames. Bright rocker panel was standard on President Classics.

Price History
(Representative models)

95+ point condition 1	1982	1987	1990	Return
1953–55 Champion/Commander sedans	$3,000	$3,600	$5,500	7.9%
1954 Conestoga wagon	2,500	3,500	5,750	11.0
1955 President State four door	3,000	4,200	5,750	8.4
1956–58 Champion/Commander sedans	2,300	3,200	4,750	9.5
1956–58 Champion/Commander wagons	2,200	3,000	5,000	10.8
1956 President Classic four door	2,600	4,200	5,600	10.1
1956–57 President wagon	2,500	3,800	5,200	9.6
1957–58 Scotsman	1,500	3,000	4,500	14.7

Gardner's new Pinehurst station wagon for 1956. Hood ornament was a variation of the ringed teardrop invented by LeBaron coachbuilders and popularized on the early postwar Buicks.

For 1957, Studebaker gave a facelift to the Gardner design with a wraparound grille and a more integrated front bumper, plus new two-tone patterns. Presidents carried a two-tone panel on the rear fender and roof.

The 1957 Commander Parkview station wagon was fitted with handsome optional bladed wheel covers.

The 1958 Studebaker line arrived with the new Scotsman sedan. There has been a recent flurry of interest in the Scotsman, perhaps because it is so homely that it deserves to be loved—even the hubcaps were devoid of chrome.

The Champion two-door sedan of 1958 showed what a difference trim made. Headlamp pods housed dual headlights as well.

Quad headlamps were used on the 1958 President four-door sedan.

A 1958 Econ-O-Miler as prepared by Studebaker for the taxi market. If I owned one of these I'd paint it taxi yellow and fit it with a meter, going all out to emphasize its special purpose.

Studebaker built its first postwar station wagon, called the Conestoga, in 1954, and continued through to 1955 as the Commander Regal. This is the 1954 model, but airbrushed V-8 emblem should be on the vent door. Conestoga is a useful little collector car for swap meet prowlers.

Chapter 19

President 1955

	Fun	Investment	Anguish
Speedster	8	6	6
Hardtop	5	7	4
Coupe	5	3	2

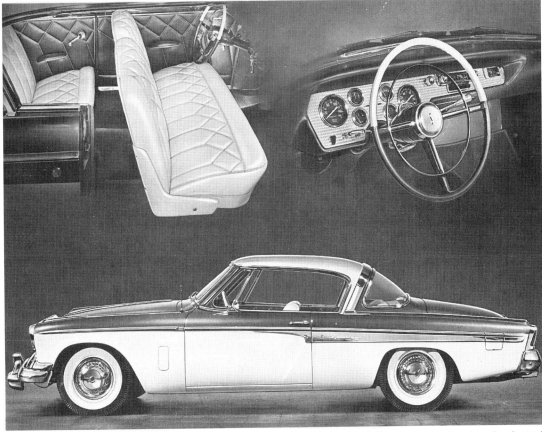

This is a standard press handout for the rakish President Speedster, showing its unique upholstery pattern, striking tooled metal dash with white-on-black instruments and wild two-tone paint scheme with standard spoke wheel covers. Speedster badge and script is on bodyside molding aft of the doors; note also the board band over the C pillar. Speedsters are big-ticket items, worth fifty percent more than comparable 1953–54 Starliners, and also much scarcer; less than 200 probably still exist.

To comprehend Studebaker's rationale behind the 1955 models we have to remember the traditional new-car lead time: three years for most of Detroit, two at the outside in Studebaker's perennial cash-poor state. In this case the 1955s were ordained in early 1953, after the handsome Loewy cars had been introduced but had failed to sell. "Our assignment then became obvious," recalls stylist Bob Bourke: "We were to lather the new cars up with chrome to compete with what management saw as the most popular cars in America—the 1953 Buicks!"

Management wasn't entirely wrong, but aesthetically what occurred on the 1955 Studebaker was reprehensible. Bourke had conceived of a hollow grille cavity formed of surrounding sheet metal on the original facelift. Basically, he got that, but he had to use a surround of chromium and plaster a big V motif in the previously empty grille. The oblong parking lamps flanking the grille cavity came off all right, but the sales department wanted such options as a gaudy hood ornament and combination bumper guard and foglamps. More chrome was applied to the body sides, destroying the elegant fuselage of 1953–54. Salespeople also influenced the 1955 color schemes, including such tasteful combinations as lemon and lime, popular on the Speedster and hardtop.

Yet we cannot say that these efforts were in vain. For the model year, Studebaker sales were almost double the 1954 total, though of course 1954 was a particularly grim time. But 1955 was the last year until the Lark's arrival (1959) that Studebaker would manage six-figure production.

What To Look For

The President, which hadn't been seen since 1942, was a pleasant revival for long-time Studebaker partisans. Top of the line and clearly the most collectible today was the President Speedster, progenitor of the Hawks and a production evolution of a short-wheelbase, two-seat sports car Bob Bourke had proposed back when the 1953 looked to set the auto world on its ear. The Speedster, which retained the long hardtop wheelbase, began life as a conventional President. It was given special badges, simulated wire wheels, heavy bumper guard and foglamps as standard, and imaginative combination paint jobs—lemon and lime, pink and grey, black and white being among the more popular. On the inside was leather and vinyl upholstery color-keyed to match the exterior and a beautiful, engine-turned dashboard with purposeful white-on-black instruments. Power steering and brakes, radio and clock, whitewalls and back-up lamps were all standard. This car will deliver 110 mph performance and turn every head at a Studebaker Drivers Club meet. But Speedsters are rare birds, usually traded quietly among friends, and it will take a lot of effort to obtain one today.

There is little reason to recommend a conventional 1955 President hardtop (rarely called Starliners this year) or a coupe over their 1953–54 counterpart, unless you like chrome or can't pay much: prices for both are far down from the Speedster level. Nevertheless, strictly from an investment standpoint the State hardtop has outperformed the Speedster over recent years, owing to the vanishing supply of Speedsters and the turning of collectors to the hitherto ignored standard hardtop.

A Speedster probably painted lemon and lime, which is hard to imagine in black and white. The heavy combination foglamps and bumper guards really ham up the front end, but can't be taken off because they were standard equipment.

Production

Speedster	2,215
State hardtop	3,468
State coupe	3,327

Identification

Grille formed by single oblong opening with modified V inserted horizontally; large square parking lights on grille under headlamps; switch key starting. All State and Speedster models have chrome window trim, chrome molding extending length of body and chrome trim on fenders above headlamps.

Specifications

Bodies: Five-passenger hardtop and five-window coupes.

Engines: Ohv V–8, 259.2 ci (3.56 x 3.25 in.), 175 bhp, 185 bhp (Speedster, optional on late Presidents).

Chassis and drivetrain: Three-speed manual transmission, overdrive or automatic optional. Independent front suspension with coil springs and tubular shocks; live rear axle with semi-elliptic leaf springs; power steering optional.

Dimensions: Length 204.5 in., wheelbase 120.5 in., weight 3,110 lb. (coupe), 3,175 lb. (hardtop), 3,301 lb. (Speedster).

Serial Numbers

Within overall President numbers: 7150001–7170827, California 7805001–7808480.

Price History

95+ point condition 1	1982	1987	1990	Return
Speedster	$8,500	$10,000	$15,000	7.4%
State hardtop	5,000	7,500	11,000	10.4
State coupe	4,500	6,500	9,500	9.8

While the Speedster gets all the attention, the President State hardtop was almost as scarce yet is much cheaper to buy. This car is one of the later versions released in early 1955, with molding extending down from roof base to wide molding just aft of doors, which determined two-tone paint treatment. (The photo is airbrushed, possibly from the earlier version.) This version would have had the 185 hp Passmaster V–8.

Chapter 20

Golden Hawk 1956-58

	Fun	Investment	Anguish
1956	6	7	8
1957–58	8	9	5
1957–58 "400"	8	10	5

The Hawks were the last Studebakers designed by Bob Bourke before the new Studebaker-Packard management wrapped up the Loewy contract and turned design over to inhouse people. Bourke, who was striving to develop an honest sporty flavor, had to contend with the manifold pressures of a desperate sales department trying to keep up with trends. To conservative management the Loewy coupes were unsuccessful has-beens; they simply refused to learn by experience that these were potentially the most explosive sellers in the stable, conversely able to add allure to the thoroughly

The 1956 Golden Hawk was the first of the breed and also the only Hawk with a Packard engine, the big 352 V–8, which made it quite nose-heavy. Tailfins were fiberglass, grafted on to keep pace with contemporary styling tastes. Despite their driveability limitations, 1956 Golden Hawks lead 1957–58 models slightly in value; they're also hard to come by.

conventional and unexciting sedan lines. In creating the Hawks, Studebaker actually invented what Lee Iacocca's creation would later receive credit for: the first pony car. The sadness was that Iacocca's Ford Mustang enjoyed a blistering success, whereas the Hawks never really sold in adequate quantities, despite being excellent road cars praised by most testers.

Top of the line in all three years was the Golden Hawk, using the most powerful engine in the fleet: a Packard Clipper 352 V-8 in 1956, a Paxton-supercharged Studebaker 289 in 1957–58. Sumptuously trimmed inside and out, the Golden Hawk was also expensive, base-priced around $3,100 and typically selling for close to $4,000—the cost of a Buick Super or, to be more embarrassing, a Corvette or Thunderbird. As a result, sales were low, and Golden Hawks are fairly scarce on the ground today.

What To Look For

The 1956 model with its Clipper engine is a nose-heavy beast given to what in my experience can only be described as final and irrevocable understeer. It plows with a vengeance, and most examples have long since settled into a pronounced front-end rake with weakened coil springs and dicey handling. The classic color scheme is gold and white; these cars are worth ten percent more than other paint schemes.

A lot of controversy exists about the 1956, even among Studebaker collectors. The 1957s and 1958s, with their blown engines, are its performance equals and much better

Golden Hawk dashboard was derived from the 1955 President Speedster, a happy idea: genuine, honest instruments including tachometer (without redline; 5000 rpm was the outer limit!) on a beautiful engine-turned-metal panel. At lower left can be seen Studebaker's famous foot-chilling direct side ventilation; right-hand mounted parking brake was said to be more convenient to most drivers.

For 1957 the Golden Hawk grew large, concave metal tailfins, which were two-toned, and adopted a supercharged Studebaker 289 V-8, which gave the same horsepower as the previous version's unblown Packard. All things considered this and the 1958 are the best of the Hawk breed—good looking, fast and entertaining to drive. Production was highest for the three years of Golden Hawk manufacture, at 4,356 worldwide.

balanced, albeit with more pronounced tailfins. Somehow, though, the fins are part of their allure, popular in the 1950s. Among these later versions look for the Golden Hawk 400, a handsome trim variant with an all-leather interior and a broad chromium swathe running up and over the roof just ahead of the backlight. Golden Hawk 400s are extremely scarce, however. The 1958 model is the scarcest of all and worth a considerable premium over comparable 1957s.

Parts are scarce for all these models, but the 1956 presents greater problems than the other two.

Production

	1956	1957	1958
Golden Hawk	4,071	4,356	878

Identification

Square egg-crate grille with dummy scoop and freestanding parking lights mounted on fenders above headlamps. For 1956: Body length chrome strip with V or check mark just aft of doors, usually dividing two-tone paint jobs; wide bright metal rocker panel trim, small tailfins. For 1957: Larger concave tailfins with two-toning confined to fin area and sometimes the top; body side bright metal molding ends on doors. For 1958: Same as 1957 but with large round Hawk emblem on lower grille; small flanking grilles contain similar pattern mesh to central grille.

Specifications

Bodies: Two-door hardtop.

Engines: Ohv V–8, 352 ci (4.00 x 3.50 in.), 275 bhp (1956); ohv V–8, 289 ci (3.56 x 3.63 in.), 275 bhp supercharged (1957–58).

Chassis and drivetrain: Three-speed manual transmission, overdrive optional 1956, standard 1957–58, automatic optional. Independent front suspension with coil springs and tubular shocks; live rear axle with semi-elliptic leaf springs.

Dimensions: Length 204 in., wheelbase 120.5 in., weight 3,360 lb. (1956), 3,400 lb. (1957), 3,470 lb. (1958).

Serial Numbers

For 1956: 6030001–6033472, California 6800001–6800601; 1957: 6100001–6104354; 1958: 610451–611330.

Studebaker-Packard was reeling at the time of the 1958 Golden Hawk and production was terrible. Only 878 of these cars were built, and for that reason they command a slight collector preference compared to the 1957s.

The 1958 Golden Hawk can be quickly distinguished by its circular central grille medallion, distinctive wheel covers and two-tone pattern on roof and tailfins. Otherwise it was much the same as 1957, though much scarcer.

Price History

95+ point condition 1	1982	1987	1990	Return
1956 Golden Hawk	$9,000	$11,000	$14,500	6.1%
1957 Golden Hawk	7,000	10,500	13,000	8.0
1958 Golden Hawk	7,000	11,000	14,000	9.1
1957–58 Golden Hawk 400	8,000	12,000	16,000	9.1

Here's a factory photo of a rare 1958, a Golden
Hawk painted a solid color. At least a few were
produced this way but not many are known.

Leather-swathed interior of a 1957 Golden Hawk
400, the most desirable Golden Hawk, but rare;
note the 400's distinctive broad band of bright
metal ahead of the rear window.

Chapter 21

Hawk Hardtops 1956–61

	Fun	Investment	Anguish
1956 Sky Hawk	8	8	5
1956 Flight Hawk	6	8	7
1957–58 Silver Hawk	6	8	7

For those who find balance and finesse as important as brute force, the Sky Hawk provides a reasonable alternative. At $500 less than the Golden Hawk when new, it was one of the best buys around. Like the Golden Hawk (but not the cheaper, coupe-bodied Power and Flight Hawks), it used finned brake drums which resisted fade. Unlike the Golden Hawk it handled well, and with 210 bhp was no slouch in performance.

Included in the Sky Hawk was a vinyl interior of luxurious design, the same tooled-metal dashboard as the Golden Hawk (tachometer optional) and much cleaner exterior styling. The Sky Hawk was, furthermore, devoid of what Bob Bourke called "those damnable fiberglass fins." It lacked the Golden Hawk's bright metal rocker panel covers and large chrome band across the rear roofline. It was subject to the same wild two-tone color combinations, though some Sky Hawks were painted in solid colors. Technically it fell into the President series and replaced what, in 1955, had been the

The 1956 Sky Hawk, a hardtop junior to the Golden Hawk, offered a blend of milder styling and a slightly less potent, unblown engine, with most of the other Golden Hawk characteristics, including machine-turned dash. Studebaker built 3,050 Sky Hawks, along with 560 Flight Hawk hardtops for the export market; a few Silver Hawk export hardtops were also built in 1957–58.

President State hardtop. A handful of export hardtops, called Flight Hawk in 1956 and Silver Hawk in 1957–58, used the same pillarless body as the Sky Hawk.

What To Look For

Solid-color Sky Hawks are no more desirable among collectors but aesthetically more pleasing. Sky Hawks with the optional 225 bhp V–8 exist but are in short supply.

During 1956–58, Studebaker built for the export market Flight and Silver Hawk six-cylinder hardtops, which are conversation pieces nowadays and, given their rarity, a good investment, although not as much fun to drive. Although I have driven for some distance a six-cylinder 1962 GT Hawk in England, I have never encountered earlier export Hawks and would be glad to hear the experiences of current owners. Flight Hawk hardtops were trimmed per normal specifications (i.e., plainly) but used the Sky Hawk's pillarless body.

Production

	1956	1957	1958
Sky Hawk hardtop	3,050		
Flight Hawk hardtop	560		
Silver Hawk hardtop		120	56

Price History
95+ point condition 1
Sky Hawk hardtop
Flight/Silver Hawk hardtop: no data; probably similar to above.

Identification

Similar to Golden Hawk but without tailfins, dummy scoops at trailing leg of body-side V molding, or wide chrome band across backlight. Usually two-toned. Export Flight and Silver Hawks share hardtop body but are more plainly trimmed and usually painted in one color.

Specifications

Bodies: Two-door hardtop.

Engines: Ohv V–8, 289 ci (3.56 x 3.63 in.), 210 bhp, 225 bhp optional (Sky Hawk). L-head six, 185.6 ci (3.00 x 4.38 in.), 101 bhp (Flight and Silver Hawk).

Chassis and drivetrain: Three-speed manual transmission, overdrive or automatic optional. Independent front suspension with coil springs and tubular shocks; live rear axle with semi-elliptic leaf springs.

Dimensions, Sky Hawk: Length 204 in., wheelbase 120.5 in., weight 3,215 lb.

Serial Numbers

Sky Hawk: Within 56H President series: 7171001–up, California 7808501–7811699.

1982	1987	1990	Return
$5,000	$7,000	$11,000	10.4%

Chapter 22

Hawk Coupes 1956–61

	Fun	Investment	Anguish
1956 Flight Hawk	5	6	3
1956 Power Hawk	6	6	3
1957–59 Silver Hawk 6 cylinder	5	5	3
1957–59 Silver Hawk V–8	6	7	3
1960–61 Hawk 6 cylinder	5	6	3
1960–61 Hawk V–8	6	7	3
1961 Hawk four-speed V–8	9	10	4

When the Hawks blossomed as a kind of sporty sub-model Studebaker, the Flight and Power Hawk were the price leaders, using the body of the old Starlight coupe. With prices starting below $2,000, these bargain Hawks sold quite well. Considerably de-trimmed compared to the Sky and Golden Hawks, they looked fairly naked when they were new, but their styling has worn better and they come off well today. From a technical standpoint their only serious styling flaw is the bodyside bright strip, which tends to fight with the original bodyside sculpture that was retained from the original 1953

Silver Hawk was derived from the old Starlight five-window couple; finless in 1956, it sprouted tailfins like the Golden Hawk's in 1957 (shown here). Two-toning was, however, distinctly different. Bladed wheel covers were optional.

design. In fact, some style-wise collectors suggest that the original 1953 coupes would have looked better had they carried Bob Bourke's classic-inspired square grille and elongated bonnet. The more practical-minded point to their strong construction, the steel B pillar adding a great deal of rigidity you don't get in the pillarless Sky and Golden Hawks.

For the tailfin era, Studebaker evolved a single Silver Hawk line, offering the model with either six or V–8 power and applying a different pattern to two-toned models. This pattern remained through 1959, after which the cars were known only as Studebaker Hawks and the six-cylinder engine was confined to the export market.

Studebaker's attention was on the Lark in 1959–60 and the Hawk survived as a highly peripheral product. But in 1961 they came through with significant improvements, including the first four-speed manual gearbox option. This, coupled with the four-barrel 225 hp engine, made the Hawk a passable grand touring car, with 0–60 sprints in ten seconds flat and a top speed approaching 120 mph. *Car and Driver* said it would "throttle down to a near idle in fourth and still pull away to over 110 mph in an inexorable whoosh . . . around smoothly paved curves the Hawk fairly zoomed . . . Cruising at 70, 75, 80 or just about any speed you dare choose is effortless." Unfortunately, the

A 1958 Silver Hawk in the uncommon monotone paint scheme—although more Silver Hawks were single color than Golden Hawks.

Aside from the circular grille emblem there was little to distinguish the 1958 from the 1957 Silver Hawk, but this 1958 is much scarcer.

The Silver Hawk returned in 1959 whereas the hardtop Golden Hawk was dropped due to production economies, since Studebaker was heavily committed at this time to the Lark. Parking lights were moved to side grilles while the upright Hawk emblem was ranged at lower right on the grille and also placed on the tailfins. Correct emblem color is black.

For 1960, Silver was dropped from name and only Hawk script remained on the tailfins. The grille emblem, now only on the tailfins, was red, and new wheel covers were adopted. Note also the chevrons on the leading end of the tailfins.

package was getting long in the tooth by contemporary standards, and a Studebaker dealership really wasn't the optimum place to sell it. Production in 1961 was the lowest in Hawk history.

What To Look For

The most important drivetrain option was the Warner Gear four-speed manual transmission (same as the Corvette's), a $188 accessory for 1961. This, coupled with the 225 hp engine, is a combination to be cherished devoutly—if you can find one. The 1961 Hawk also benefitted from contoured bucket seats, available in cloth or vinyl. Altogether it was the best Hawk yet and, with or without the four-speed transmission, is recommended for collectors to whom

Production

	1956	1957	1958	1959	1960	1961
Flight Hawk	4,389					
Power Hawk	7,095					
Silver Hawk 6		4,163	2,442	2,417	227*	266*
Silver Hawk V-8 259		1,180	367	5,371		
Silver Hawk V-8 289		9,607	4,485		4,280	3,663

*Export only

driving is still part of a car's allure.

Studebaker temporarily dropped its most powerful 289 V–8 in 1959, so the 1959 Hawk is the least sprightly, though examples may be found with the optional power pack (four-barrel, dual exhausts). All 1960–61 Hawks, and most 1957s, used the 289 engine.

Identification

For 1956: Identifying script on decklid; body same as 1953–54 Starlight coupe from firewall back, except for bodyside bright molding from front fender to aft of doors. For 1957: Same basic body but 1953–54 body-side crease lines eliminated and large concave tailfins installed. For 1958: Same as 1957 plus large circular Hawk emblem centered on the lower grille. For 1959: Parking lamps moved from fender tops to outer ends of small flanking grilles. Chrome-on-black Hawk emblem on lower left main grille. For 1960: Grille emblem dropped, tailfin emblems now chrome-on-red; three small hash marks on leading end of tailfins. Wheelcover spokes on white-painted background. For 1961: color flash bordered by bright metal on sides under tailfins; wheelcover spokes on black-painted background.

Specifications

Bodies: Five-passenger five-window coupe.

Engines: L-head six, 185.6 ci (3.00 x 4.38 in.), 101 bhp (Flight Hawk, 1957–58 Silver Hawk six); 169.6 ci (3.00 x 4.00 in.), 90 bhp (1959–60 six), 112 bhp (1961 six). Ohv V–8, 259.2 ci (3.56 x 3.25 in.), 170–185 bhp (Power Hawk), 180–195 bhp (1957–59 Silver Hawk); ohv V–8, 289.0 ci (3.56 x 3.63 in.), 210–225 bhp (1957–58 Silver Hawk, 1960–61 Hawk).

The final appearance for the pillar-body Hawk coupe was 1961, when the four-speed gearbox was also offered. These cars are distinguished by their double chrome fender molding, usually enclosing a contrasting color. Wheel cover paint went from white to black; Hawk script was shifted forward on the fenders. Four-speed versions of this model are desirable and worth seeking out.

Chassis and drivetrain: Three-speed manual transmission, overdrive and automatic optional, four-speed manual optional 1961. Independent front suspension with coil springs and tubular shocks; live rear axle with semi-elliptic leaf springs.

Dimensions: Length 204 in., wheelbase 120.5 in., weight 2,780 lb. (Flight Hawk) to 3,210 lb. (Silver Hawk).

Serial Numbers

For 1956–58: Within Champion/Commander series. For 1959–61: Within Lark VI/VIII series, 1961 Hawk engine number from P74701-up.

Price History

95+ point condition 1	1982	1987	1990	Return
1956 Flight Hawk	$3,750	$5,500	$ 7,000	8.1%
1956 Power Hawk	5,000	6,000	8,500	6.9
1957–59 Silver Hawk 6	4,000	5,000	7,000	7.2
1957–59 Silver Hawk V–8	5,000	7,000	9,500	8.4
1960–61 Hawk V–8	4,500	7,000	9,000	9.1
1961 Hawk V–8 (225 hp, four speed)	5,500	8,000	12,000	10.2

Chapter 23

Starlight 1958

Hardtop	Fun 4	Investment 5	Anguish 4

With Studebaker-Packard reeling, its survival hinging on the make-or-break 1959 Lark, promotion for the 1958 line was kept to a minimum (though some lovely line art was commissioned for the inexpensive black-and-white display ad campaign). Most brochures were single-sheet broadsides for dealer use. The model lineup was greatly rationalized, especially with regard to station wagons and the shorter-wheelbase Presidents, which hadn't sold well. The President was putting in its last appearance this year, its long history dating back to 1926.

But one body style was new: the Starlight, Studebaker's first hardtop not based on a Raymond Loewy design. "This was a fairly nice workout," designer Duncan McRae says, "bearing a roof and backlight astonishingly similar to the concurrent DeSotos. There's no truth to the rumor that we bor-

Odd-model-out was the unique Starlight hardtop, a single year body style introduced in 1958 and rendered extinct by the new Lark the following year. This is the upper-level President model, rarer and with a longer wheelbase than the Commander, with various President trim bits as standard, including, of course, quad headlamps. Styled in a hurry by Duncan McRae, the Starlight had an elegant roofline.

rowed a DeSoto for templates—sizes are different—but it did have an impact on our thinking."

At a time of great financial trauma the Starlight was the only indication of pork in the Studebaker-Packard budget. It came as a Commander or President, priced to compete with rivals from the Big Three. Less than 4,000 were built, with about three-quarters going to the domestic market. Promotions called it the "Scintillating Studebaker," but it evidently did not scintillate enough to tempt many buyers.

What To Look For

The 1958 Starlight is such an oddball that it has to be considered in a separate chapter, but finding one won't be easy, since the low production rate has caused most to be spoken for years ago. The preferable model is the President, but that comprised under one-third of production. Look for bright two-tone paint jobs (original colors, of course), and avoid anything bearing the slightest indication of rust. Starlights tend to be well optioned, and you might find such useful items as power seats/steering/windows and air conditioning.

Production

Commander Starlight	2,555
President Starlight	1,171

Identification

Only pillarless body style other than Hawk in 1958 line. Massive bar grille and quad headlamps in bulbous housings. President version carries nameplate on rear fender. With the sedan of that year, the top-line Starlight was the last Studebaker President.

Specifications

Bodies: Two-door hardtop.

Engines: Ohv V–8, 259.2 ci (3.56 x 3.25 in.), 180 bhp (Commander); 289.0 ci 3.56 x 3.63 in.), 225 bhp (President).

Chassis and drivetrain: Three-speed manual transmission, overdrive or automatic optional. Independent front suspension with coil springs and tubular shocks; live rear axle with semi-elliptic leaf springs.

Dimensions: Length 202.4 in., President 206.4 in.; wheelbase 116.5 in., President 120.5 in.; weight 3,270 lb., President 3,355 lb.

Serial Numbers

Part of 1958 Commander and President series.

Price History
95+ point condition 1

	1982	1987	1990	Return
Commander Starlight	$2,500	$3,500	$5,000	9.1%
President Starlight	3,000	4,000	6,000	9.1

Chapter 24

Lark 1959–62

	Fun	Investment	Anguish
Convertible	7	6	5
Hardtop	5	4	5
Sedans and wagons	2	1	5

Had it not been for the Lark, Studebaker would have died around 1960. As carefully laid as a product plan from General Motors, the Lark was produced in record time from largely off-the-shelf components, yet was novel enough to look different and take precise advantage of the public mood, which had then shifted from chrome-laden land yachts to economical compacts. Studebaker didn't actually plan it that way; it guessed. But for once in its life it guessed right. On sales of $387 million the firm earned over $28 million—the first profitable year since 1953 and the most profit in anyone's memory.

Its concept may be credited to Harold Churchill, an experienced and longtime South Bend manager who replaced Roy Hurley after the disastrous period of Curtiss-Wright management in 1956–57. Remembering history, "Church" showed old films of the 1939 Champion to his minions, telling them, "That's the kind of car we need." That Churchill could sense such a role for Studebaker when the American market was still demanding lower, longer, wider and heavier cars makes him a wizard to rank with

Slotted side grilles identified the original 1959 Lark, the most desirable model of which is the Regal hardtop, produced in about equal numbers with six and V-8 engines. The eight-cylinder versions have increased in value rapidly during the last five or six years and are no longer the bargains they once were. Model year is an insignificant factor.

For 1960, the side grilles adopted the main grille mesh pattern and the Lark emblem moved to the lower grille center. Engines were designated in Roman numerals; this is a Lark VI Deluxe four-door sedan.

George Romney of American Motors, who was also gambling on a concentrated small-car effort around the same time.

Designed by Duncan McRae and a team including Bob Doehler, Ted Pietsch, Virgil Exner, Jr., and others, the stubby Lark body was hung around the previous (1953–58) body's inner shell by Studebaker's resourceful chief engineer, Gene Hardig. The main dimensional difference between the Lark and its predecessors was front and rear overhang. Considering Studebaker-Packard's limited finances, what these people created was ingenious—not a single car, but an entire line: two-door sedans, four-door sedans, wagons, hardtops and, by 1960, convertibles, with a V-8 option for the top-end Lark Regal.

Meanwhile, the economy obligingly dovetailed into recession. People went shopping for small, cheap cars and found nothing at Big Three dealerships; they ventured into Studebaker showrooms (unaccustomed territory for most of them) and found...Larks! Production tripled, and Studebaker rose from fourteenth to eleventh in the 1959 production race; they hadn't done that well since 1953.

What To Look For

In terms of investment, Larks have performed better than you might expect, appreciating in value at a rate often faster than more desirable earlier Studebakers like the Loewy coupes and Golden Hawks. The most desirable model is the convertible, which debuted in 1960, but the V-8 is preferable to the six-cylinder version and the best of all is the 1962 Daytona, with contoured seats (recliner optional), a front console and sporty color-keyed interiors. Next best is the hardtop, which, like the convertible, was available strictly as a Lark Regal until 1962, when a Daytona hardtop arrived with a (collector-desirable) sunroof. Daytonas carry a walnut grain instrument panel, pile carpeting and vinyl door panels.

The 1962 was also the first model with the Warner Gear four-speed option in Larks; the lever was placed properly amidships on the floor, but had a long throw and a rather wispy feel. Nicest sedan is the Cruiser, another reincarnation of the old Land Cruiser, on the longer station wagon wheelbase. Normally, Lark V-8s were the 259 variety, but the 289 was optional on the 1962 Daytona and Cruiser, with either the normal 210 or Power Pack 225. For collectors of oddities, there were panel truck conversions of Lark wagons (with blind panels aft of the doors), and a bare-bones Utility Sedanette two door with no rear seat to compete for the austerity market like the Scotsman had in the past. The Econ-O-Miler, later referred to as Heavy-Duty, was an extended four-door sedan, usually produced as taxicabs and finally, in 1962, used strictly for cab purposes.

A Lark VIII four-door wagon. The VIII designation denoted the V-8 engine.

New for 1960, the Lark convertible came as a six or V-8; this is the only year in which the ragtop was in good supply, and the vast majority seen today are 1960s. After that, production tapered off in a hurry. Eights outnumbered sixes.

Compare this 1961 convertible with the 1960 models: quad headlamps incorporating parking lights, simpler grille texture and black-trimmed wheel covers were the main changes. But production was well down and only about 2,000 1961s were built. This photo also shows the correct backlight pattern.

Novel for its time was the folding Skytop factory sunroof on the 1961 Lark hardtop. Hardtop volume also plummeted on these body styles as Big Three compact competition bit into Studebaker's Lark market. Clean examples are difficult to find.

Production

	1959	1960	1961	1962*
Lark VI:				
Deluxe four-door sedan	22,566	22,534	15,891	22,400
Regal four-door sedan	11,898	5,524	3,802	5,350
Regal Cruiser four-door sedan			24	
Deluxe two-door sedan	33,259	24,605	12,571	16,600
Regal two-door hardtop†	7,075	2,829	1,870	4,500
Regal convertible†		3,107	979	1,300
Deluxe four-door wagon		5,420	2,924	4,200
Regal four-door wagon		1,925	693	1,000
Deluxe two-door wagon	13,227	3,497	1,210	
Regal two-door wagon	5,685			
Econ-O-Miler/HD four-door sedan	1,033	1,096	1,108	1,850
Lark VIII:				
Deluxe four-door sedan	1,367	14,231	7,343	4,000
Regal four-door sedan	14,530	11,410	3,202	4,500
Regal Cruiser four door			5,232	7,400
Deluxe two-door sedan	550	8,102	2,003	2,600
Regal two-door hardtop†	7,996	4,565	1,666	4,000
Regal convertible†		5,464	1,002	1,400
Deluxe four-door wagon		5,711	1,815	2,600
Regal four-door wagon		5,741	1,851	2,700
Deluxe two-door wagon	378	1,734	1,177	
Regal two-door wagon	7,419			
Econ-O-Miler/HD/taxi four-door sedan	92	215	222	350

*1962 production figures in preceding table are rounded-off estimates based on six-cylinder versus V-8 sales in 1961, since exact breakdowns are not known to exist. Including both sixes and V-8s, Studebaker reported the following 1962 production: 49,961 four-door sedans, 19,196 two-door sedans, 8,480 hardtops, 10,522 four-door wagons, 2,681 convertibles, 2,212 taxis.

† Includes Daytona hardtop and convertible in 1961–62.

Identification

For 1959: Square grille of horizontal bars with Hawk emblem at lower right. For 1960: Mesh grille with Lark emblem at lower center. For 1961: Lark emblem at lower right on grille; Regal models received quad headlamps. For 1962: Major facelift with squarer greenhouse and Mercedes-style mesh grille divided into twelve sections by three horizontal and two vertical bars; quad headlamps; round taillights. Daytonas carry wide side moldings with Daytona script.

Specifications

Bodies: Four- and two-door sedans and wagons, two-door hardtops and convertibles.

Engines: Lark VI: L-head six, 169.6 ci (3.00 x 4.00 in.), 90 bhp (1959-60), 112 bhp (1961-62). Lark VIII: ohv V-8, 259.2 ci (3.56 x 3.25 in.), 180-195 bhp (1959-62); ohv V-8, 289 ci (3.56 x 3.63 in.), 210-225 bhp (optional 1962 Cruiser and Daytona).

Chassis and drivetrain: Three-speed manual transmission, overdrive automatic optional, four-speed optional 1962. Independent front suspension with coil springs and tubular shocks; live rear axle with semi-elliptic leaf springs.

Dimensions: Length 175 in. (1959–61), 184 in. (1959–61 wagons, long sedans), 188 in. (1962), 184 in. (1962 two doors), 187 in. (1962 wagons); wheelbase 108.5 in. (1959–61), 109 in. (1962 two doors), 113 in. (1959 Regal wagon, 1960–62 wagons, long sedans); weight 2,577 lb. (base two door) to 3,315 lb. (convertibles).

Serial Numbers

Prefixes begin with model year (59, 60, 61, 62) followed by letters: S for sixes (SC Canada), V for V-8s (VC Canada). V-8 Engine numbers: V418701, Canada VC14701 (1959); V454701, Canada VC16701 (1960); V510401, Canada VC18501 (1961); V534910, Canada VC19601 (1962 259 ci); P79801, Canada P2801 (1962 289 ci).

Daytona package for 1961 included bucket seats with the console, wood-tone instrument panel and more luxurious interior trim. The Warner Gear four speed, its selector sprouting from the transmission tunnel, was available with V-8s.

Riding the longer 113 in. wheelbase, the Lark Cruiser revived the old Land Cruiser theme, offering extra legroom for backseat passengers.

Cruisers were plentiful; ninety-nine percent of them were V-8s and a six would be a rare find, but nobody cares.

Price History

95+ point condition 1	1982	1987	1990	Return
Sedans	$2,000	$3,000	$ 4,500	10.7%
Wagons	1,500	2,500	4,500	14.7
Regal hardtop V–8	3,000	5,000	7,000	11.2
Regal convertible V–8	4,000	8,000	10,000	12.1
1962 Daytona hardtop V–8	4,500	6,000	8,000	7.5
1962 Daytona convertible V–8	5,500	9,000	11,000	9.1

Note: Deduct ten percent for six-cylinder hardtops and convertibles.

By removing the snap-out commercial panels, the Lark Panel-Wagon converts to a regular two-door station wagon. This is a neat little rig, not commonly seen, but usually available for a song when it comes up for sale. It needs white-walls, wheel covers and a Studebaker logo on the panel to shine at meets.

A facelift was urgently needed by 1962, but there was little money. Brooks Stevens applied a Mercedes-like grille and stubby stand-up hood ornament, altered body creases and rear deck, doing wonders with a negligible budget. His effort did help sales recover somewhat that year, and even convertible sales improved: 2,700 were built, about evenly divided between sixes and V–8s. Parking lights were amber for the first time in 1962.

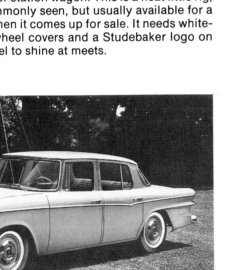

The long-wheelbase Lark Cruiser. All Cruisers were V–8s in 1962 and remain in fairly good supply.

A rear-end view of the Lark Cruiser showing Stevens' rear-end facelift: round taillights and block letters on the trunklid.

A 1962 Lark four-door wagon offered 72 cu. ft. of luggage space, optional third seat and roof luggage rack.

Chapter 25

Gran Turismo Hawk 1962–64

	Fun	Investment	Anguish
Gran Turismo Hawk	9	9	5

Brooks Stevens' remarkable facelift of the old Loewy coupe brought wide acclaim, and deservedly so. Most people never thought it was coming—rumor was that the 1961 Hawk would be the last of its kind—and to see the crisp, new Gran Turismo rise phoenixlike out of the tired old coupe body was a genuine surprise. Equally notable was the speed with which it went from concept to completion: "I built the first handmade car in Milwaukee in June," Stevens says, "and we had it in front of dealers in September."

The GT Hawk involved a new greenhouse, square and formal, frankly patterned after the Thunderbird's; smooth new body sides with a front-to-rear bright metal cap like concurrent Lincoln Continentals; a classic style grille with a "false grille" appliqué out back (to disguise the decklid, which dated back to 1956); and a new interior with bucket seats and a handsome dashboard grouping white-on-black instruments in a concave binnacle ahead of the driver. High-carpeted doors, a hidden radio speaker, perforated vinyl headlining and the 289 V-8 were standard (some export models were sixes); reclining front buckets, four-speed gearbox, air conditioning and power windows, steering and brakes were optional. The Hawk was base-priced at just over $3,000 and usually sold for around $4,000 equipped, a shade high for a Studebaker—and this resulted in lower sales than it deserved. But the car did give the Hawk a new lease on life and, had Studebaker sur-

vived, Stevens had wonderful ideas for future Hawks waiting in the wings.

What to Look For

A decade ago the scarcer 1964 model had a twenty-five percent lead in value over the 1962–63 GTs, but this has not held, although all three models have increased reasonably in value, as have the R1/R2 Super Hawks. Unlike a lot of high-blown muscle cars, the latter have not been subject to hype and forgeries, as have, say Pontiac GTOs. If you

What Brooks Stevens did with the 1962 Gran Turismo Hawk was little short of miraculous. On a miniscule budget, he transformed the old Hawk and brought it right up to date, with a Thunderbird-style roofline and bold traditional grille, a minimum of brightwork and elegant surface development. This is a retouched photo of Stevens' prototype, which had round parking lights, but is otherwise completely stock.

can find a GT, it is a good buy for the performance enthusiast.

On 1962 models, the 225 hp four-barrel V-8 and the four-speed gearbox are highly desirable, adding at least twenty-five percent to a GT's value versus a comparable standard model. Reclining seats, power windows and air conditioning are rare accessories. Be extremely careful on 1962s to check the condition of the vinyl seat inserts. These have thin scorings to simulate pleats which are too thin and wear out, and new-old-

Inside the GT Stevens crafted an aircraft-style cockpit with crash padding and recessed controls; instruments were placed on an angled panel, later aped by Thunderbird, from whom Brooks had borrowed the GT's roofline! Notoriously weak pleated upholstery of the 1962 Hawk is visible on door panel at left.

GT facelift for 1963 duplicated the Lark-style grille (but with smaller squares), eliminated chrome headlamp rims and added a tricolor emblem to the doors. Production was cut in half, however, as Studebaker sales took their final plunge. The R2 Avanti engine was available on some 1963s, known as Super Hawks.

Final production GT—and the scarcest by far—was the 1964 model, with half-vinyl roof, new wheel covers and a minor trim reshuffle, including the Hawk badge in the grille center. This car also bears an R2 badge at lower right on the grille. The improved pleated upholstery of the 1964 can be seen inside.

The most noticeable change on the 1964 was the clean decklid, the old metal appliqué being shorn off and a new red, white and blue round medallion and script being added. The exhaust deflectors, common to late-model Studebakers, are high-demand items; exhaust actually exits from a large hole underneath.

stock does not exist. (The original appearance can be simulated by installing new vinyl which has been prepleated by folding or stitching.)

Among 1963–64 models, the most important are the Super Hawks, with the Avanti R1 and R2 engines; although 1964 Super Hawks were technically available with the even more potent R3 and R4 engines, none are known to have been built. Contrary to the usual rule of thumb, GTs look best and sell best in dark colors, black and maroon being among the more desirable. The 1963–64 models do not suffer from the failure of seat material, and the 1964 has the nicest buckets, but the 1964 also has full-width dashboard woodgraining that suffers badly from discoloration and is hard to duplicate if it must be replaced.

The dashboard of the 1964 retained the previous pattern but the instruments were arrayed over a matte black surface, with woodgraining instead of metal on the panel to the right.

Production

	1962	1963	1964
GT Hawk	9,335	4,634	1,767

Identification

For 1962: Gran Turismo gold script on doors, large square grille with wide chrome collar; small flanking openings carry oblong parking lights. For 1963: Tricolor badge next to Gran Turismo on doors and on grille; new grille mesh duplicated in flanking openings which now carry round, amber parking lights. For 1964: Vertical Hawk emblem in center of grille; stand-up hood ornament; decklid appliqué removed and deck smoothed off.

Specifications

Bodies: Two-door hardtop.

Engines: Ohv V–8, 289 ci (3.56 x 3.63 in.), 210 bhp, 225 bhp optional with four-barrel carburetor and dual exhausts. Optional R1 Avanti engine, 289 ci, solid lifters, four-barrel carburetor, 10.25:1 compression, 240 bhp; optional supercharged R2 Avanti engine, 289 ci, 290 bhp. L-head six or 259 V–8 fitted to some export models.

Chassis and drivetrain: Three-speed manual transmission, overdrive, four-speed manual and automatic optional. Independent front suspension with coil springs and tubular shocks; live rear axle with semi-elliptic leaf springs.

Dimensions: Length 204 in., wheelbase 120.5 in., weight 3,230 lb. (1962), 3,280 lb. (1963), 3,120 lb. (1964).

Serial Numbers

For 1962: 62V1001–up, Canada 62VC1002–up; 1963: 63V1001–up, Canada 63VC1001–up; 1964: 64V1001–up, Canada 64VC1001–up; not consecutive: part of Lark series.

Price History

95+ point condition 1

	1982	1987	1990	Return
1962 GT Hawk	$4,500	$ 7,500	$10,000	10.5%
1963 GT Hawk	5,000	8,500	11,000	10.4
1964 GT Hawk	5,500	9,000	11,500	11.0
1963–64 Super Hawk R1	6,500	10,500	13,000	9.1
1963–64 Super Hawk R2	7,500	12,000	15,000	9.1

Chapter 26

Passenger Cars 1963–64

	Fun	Investment	Anguish
Convertible	7	6	5
Hardtop	5	4	5
Wagonaire	7	2	7
Sedans and wagons	2	1	5

Studebaker began downplaying the Lark name in 1963 (billing Cruiser as a separate entity) because it was no longer an advantage: the squared-off body now dated back to 1959 in its basic form, and in construction to the mists of prehistory (1953) in automotive terms. Studebaker lacked the money to do much about it. All-new families of sedans were being conjured up by both Brooks Stevens and Raymond Loewy, but no one really had much confidence that they'd ever see production—and they didn't.

Meanwhile, the old bodies struggled on with whatever stylists could do to make them new-looking. Primarily, this was

The new 1963 dashboard and upholstery detail are visible. The Wagonaire was eminently practical, enabling almost any load to be carried; but aging seals have often let in rain and corrosion is a problem on many of these cars today.

Brooks Stevens' imaginative new Wagonaire with its sliding roof section: the first station wagon able to carry tall trees and small giraffes with dexterity. Wagonaires were available from the stripped Standard on up to the luxurious Daytona series, but sales were slumping so fast now that they didn't make much of a difference. (Fixed-roof wagons were a delete option on Standards.) Disk brakes were a worthwhile new option in 1963, as were the Avanti R1 and R2 engines, which were offered in tandem with various Avanti suspension and powertrain features from mid 1963. Technically available was the supercharged 335 hp R3 V–8 (fitted to a single Commander two door along with nine Avantis in 1964) and the unblown 280 hp R4 V–8 (fitted to a lone Daytona hardtop).

What to Look For

These final cars from South Bend have appreciated more rapidly than all comparable postwar models during the past ten years, probably because of their being the last, and because the generation that remembers them is in its peak earning years. (This is true for many other makes: the 1960s are hot, the 1950s and 1970s less so.) The Cruiser, which could hardly be given away in 1980, has increased notably in value, although my choice would still be the Daytona convertible, on general principles.

R1 and R2 Super Hawks are the most desirable cars from this group and command a substantial premium over normal V–8s.

Wagonaires are eminently practical for swap meet denizens but not much in demand—and subject to torrential water leaks, resulting in rust where you don't expect it, even on Studebakers. Daytona four-speeds—convertibles and sunroof hardtops especially—are the most sought-after conventional models, but production was scanty, especially in 1964. And look at those convertible numbers!

Production

	1963	1964
Four-door sedans	40,113	27,289
Two-door sedans	17,401	8,315
Hardtops	3,763	2,414
Convertibles	1,015	703
Four-door wagons	11,915	5,163
Taxicabs	1,170	455

Identification

For 1963: Mercedes-style grille divided into more and smaller oblong sections than 1962; stubby stand-up hood ornament. For 1964: full-width inverted trapezoid grille and stand-up "S-in-circle" hood ornament (not spring-loaded—don't lean on it). Recontoured, higher hood and decklines with rectangular taillights mounted over backup lights high on the rear end.

Specifications

Bodies: Four- and two-door sedan, four-door station wagon (with and without sliding roof section), hardtop, convertible.

Engines: L-head six, 169.6 ci (3.00 x 4.00 in.), 112 bhp (all six-cylinder models); ohv V-8, 259.6 ci (3.56 x 3.25 in.), 180–195 bhp (all V-8s save Cruiser); 289 ci (3.56 x 3.63 in.), 210–225 bhp (Cruiser, optional other

Daytonas were the top of the wagon line in 1963, with the Wagonaire sliding rear roof sections, another inspiration of designer Brooks Stevens.

Sunroof Daytona of 1963, showing the notoriously ill-wearing scored vinyl seat inserts, also used on the GT Hawk.

The Cruiser continued for 1963. These cars have experienced relatively large increases in value since the mid 1980s, among the highest of any Studebaker; yet they are still available in fine condition for little more than $5,000. Avoid rust at all costs.

Last of the convertibles was the 1964 Daytona. The production run was merely 703, and they are now worth up to $10,000 on the collector market. Bucket seats, performance options, including four-speed transmission, and the best upholstery yet fitted to a Lark-type Studebaker make the 1964 Daytona ragtop highly desirable. It is worth a premium compared to the 1963 version.

The Daytona Wagonaire for 1964. A low-production wagon in short supply, it is probably the most collectible station wagon in the postwar period. Inverted trapezoidal grille and stand-up hood ornament were Brooks Stevens' design touches.

The R4 304.5 ci Avanti engine installed in a 1964 Studebaker Daytona hardtop. This was the only R4 factory installation.

Another Daytona hardtop, this one an R2, as identified by badge on front fender.

models), 240 bhp (R1 Super Lark), supercharged 290 bhp (R2 Super Lark).

Chassis and drivetrain: Three-speed manual transmission, overdrive, four-speed manual and automatic optional. Independent front suspension with coil springs and tubular shocks; live rear axle with semi-elliptic leaf springs.

Dimensions: Length 190 in., wagons 193 in., Cruiser 194 in.; wheelbase 113 in., two-door models 109 in.; weight 2,650 lb. (standard two-door sedan) to 3,490 lb. (Daytona Wagonaire); convertibles 3,300 lb., hardtops 3,100 lb.

Serial Numbers
For 1963: 63V1001–up, Canada 63VC1001–up; 1964: 64V1001–up, Canada 64VC1001–up; shared with GT Hawk.

Price History

95+ point condition 1	1982	1987	1990	Return
Sedans and wagons	$2,000	$3,000	$ 5,000	12.1%
Cruiser	2,000	4,000	6,500	15.9
Daytona hardtop	3,500	6,000	8,000	10.9
Daytona convertible	5,500	8,500	10,000	7.7

Note: Add fifteen percent for R1 engine, twenty-five percent for R2 engine.

Chapter 27

Avanti 1963–64

	Fun	Investment	Anguish
R1	8	8	5
R2	9	10	7
R3	10	10	9

All that romantic guff you've heard so often about Raymond Loewy's creation of the Avanti is mainly true. In February 1961, responding to a request from Studebaker president Sherwood Egbert, Loewy sent Egbert a portfolio of his automotive designs.

The project was authorized on March 22 (according to Egbert) or March 9 (according to Loewy), in clandestine desert surroundings near Palm Springs, California. Here Loewy brought designers Tom Kellogg and Bob Andrews and his studio vice president

Raymond Loewy, Sherwood Egbert and the 1963 Avanti: an airbrushed publicity photo showing script that varies from production. This photo reveals the dramatic lowness of the car; its imaginative styling is still attractive by today's standards, and original Avantis remain among the greatest performance bargains in the 1960s field.

Interim 1963 Avanti with round headlamps but later grille over front air intake; this is badged as an R2 on front fender.

John Ebstein. These four men really did create the essential clay model, which they sent to South Bend on April 27.

Back home in Indiana, designer Bob Doehler led a team of stylists in finalizing the full-size model, while chief engineer Gene Hardig and his colleagues made the concept work on a Lark convertible frame, which wasn't easy. This was hardly the basis of the sporting gran turismo Egbert envisioned, and certain liberties had to be taken, like placing the seats far to the rear for optimum weight distribution. Sway bars and rear radius rods were needed to keep the car on the ground. Also, Egbert wanted a fiberglass body to save time and money, but Hardig persuaded him to farm that job out to the Molded Fiber Glass (MFG) company in Ohio, rather than creating a new fiberglass department at South Bend. (Engineer Otto Klausmeyer says that he convinced Egbert by telling him that a fiberglass-producing Studebaker plant would look "like the inside of a flour mill.")

Whether you liked or loathed the Avanti was a matter of taste. "Great liberties have been taken merely to achieve the effect," said *Road & Track*, whose tastes lay elsewhere. "The styling is contrived, straining for visual impact to the exclusion of utility, or efficiency, or grace." But the Avanti was a dramatic and unique design, and in the years since it has worn well—testified to by the fact that a descendant is still in production three decades later.

The Avanti was designed to wheedle customers back into ominously empty Studebaker showrooms, and ultimately to spark a new generation of new passenger cars. But in the end, the Avanti's bright prospects were shattered by the company itself.

The first 100 MFG bodies were hopelessly botched: doors wouldn't close, hoods were out of line, fenders were mismatched. "When we tried to drop the rear window into position it fell through the hole," said Klausmeyer. Hasty fixes were applied. Some worked, some never did, and Avanti quality remained mixed for the duration of its run. This was not all MFG's fault—they'd been making satisfactory Corvette bodies for a decade—but the result of Egbert's unrealis-

A 1964 Avanti R3, displaying some of the physical changes that were phased in: square headlamps, grille over air intake, chromed drip rails. Only nine R3s were built; this one is probably R5237, the second example produced.

tic crash program to get the Avanti into production. Granted, this enthusiastic young president was an industry newcomer and desperate for something—anything—that might restore South Bend's lagging fortunes. But to go from rough concept to mass production inside of eighteen months would have taxed even General Motors. It simply couldn't be done. Dying of cancer, poor Egbert resigned in November 1963. Studebaker as a South Bend autobuilder continued for exactly one month.

The Avanti will remain famous and respected for what it did accomplish in such a short life: twenty-nine new stock car records under the direction of Andy Granatelli at Bonneville, including the American and National Closed Car Division records of the US Auto Club for the five- and ten-kilometer and five- and ten-mile standing start; and for the one-, five- and ten-kilometer and one-, five- and ten-mile flying start. In October 1963, Bill Burke set an E-Supercharged class record (147.36 mph) driving a Paxton-blown 289 ci Avanti with Weber cam, oversize valves and Schiefer clutch and flywheel. At the same time Sherwood Egbert became the fastest American auto company president in history (a record I'm sure he still holds) by personally driving one of Granatelli's R3s to 168 mph, a fraction short of the record.

Incidentally, a street-stock Avanti R1 will deliver 0–60 mph in seven to eight seconds, the standing quarter mile in 17.5 seconds at 78 mph and a top speed of 115 mph; and an R2 will score six to seven seconds, sixteen seconds and 120 mph for those feats, respectively. And the Avanti's slick shape had a drag coefficient in the high 0.30s—we're still trying to break 0.30 today at a time when your workaday Pontiac had a Cd of around 0.55. Those are pretty good numbers for what some called "a Lark in a gilded cage."

What to Look For

Avanti was the only Studebaker to come standard with the R1 engine: ¾ race cam, heavy-duty valves and crankshaft bearings, dual breaker distributor, viscous fan drive, four-barrel carburetor and dual exhaust. Likewise, it was the only R1-equipped Studebaker available with air conditioning, so factory air should be high on your list of desirable options. The rest of the list: power windows and power steering (both years), chrome wire wheels and tilt steering wheel (1964). Chrome wires in mint condition add about $2,000 to an Avanti's value.

Andy Granatelli and Paxton provided the supercharger for the R2 engine, which developed 1 hp per ci on the long-running 289 V-8. Granatelli also developed three more powerful engines bored out to 304.5 ci, the R3, R4 and R5, but only the R3 was seen in production (nine Avantis and one Commander), boasting at least 45 hp more than the R2. The R3s were all 1964 models, equipped with AM radios, Firestone 500 nylon tires and either power steering or the optional quick-steering manual set-up with 16:1 steering ratio. One car had black tires and the adjustable wheel; the rest had whitewalls and the conventional steering column. Three even had electric window lifts. No production Avantis had R4 and R5 engines, which were really experimental.

Avanti owners have various preferences between the "1963" model (generally speaking with round headlamps and no mesh in its radiator opening) and the "1964" model (square headlamp bezels, grille mesh, woodgrain interior accents). There is also a lot of confusion, since some round-headlamp cars came with grille mesh and some 1963s had woodgrain. The solid vinyl upholstery of the later cars seems better looking and more durable than the perforated style of the early ones.

In terms of value, Avantis should appeal even to the flinty-hearted investors as opposed to the car enthusiasts—or more realistically to enthusiasts thinking of investment. In January 1990, a panel of market analysts convened by *Automotive Investor* newsletter chose the Avanti as one of its best buys for the year, and indeed for the long term, predicting value increases from twenty-five to seventy-five percent through the year 2000, although Avantis haven't risen spectacularly in the past. While the latter-day Avanti—one resists calling it a replicar—sells new for $60,000 and is worth at least $25,000 used, condition 3 originals were trading for four-figure prices at the beginning of 1990 and show-quality originals could be had for $15,000 to $20,000.

Production

	1963	1964
R1/R2 round headlight	3,834	50
R1/R2 square headlight		750
R3		9

See note on engineering prototypes under specifications below.

Identification

Unmistakable Coke-bottle fuselage. All 1963 models have round headlamps, empty radiator intake; all 1964 models plus fifty 1963s have square headlamps. All R3s are 1964 models.

Specifications

Bodies: Fiberglass two-door, four-passenger coupe.

Engines: Ohv V-8, 289 ci (3.56 x 3.63 in.), 240 bhp; R2 supercharged, 285-290 bhp. Ohv V-8, 304.5 ci (3.65 x 3.63 in.), supercharged, 335 (official) to as much as 400 bhp (R3). Ohv V-8, 304.5 ci (3.65 x 3.63 in.), twin superchargers, about 575 bhp (experimental R5). No production Avantis with R4 or R5 engines.

Chassis and drivetrain: Three-speed manual, automatic and four-speed manual

Interior of the 1964 Avanti was much improved over the original, with woodgrain accents, solid-color vinyl trim and woodgrained steering wheel. Most of these interior bits and pieces are difficult to find, so be sure nothing's missing when you buy your Avanti.

optional, all with floor shift selectors. Independent front suspension with coil springs and tubular shocks; live rear axle with semi-elliptic leaf springs.

Dimensions: Length 192 in., wheelbase 109 in., weight 3,140 lb. (1963), 3,195 lb. (1964).

Serial Numbers

For 1963: R1001-R4834; 1964: R4835-R5643. R1 engines are identified by engine number R1001-up; R2 by engine number RS1001-up.

At least five engineering prototypes bore the special numbers EX2942 and EX2944 through EX2947. Serial numbers of the last four begin at R5650, suggesting as many as ten specials serialed after the final production car (R5643).

Avanti Running Changes

July 1962: Improved rear-window fastening.

September 1962: Revised rear shock absorbers.

October 1962: Baffled mufflers available.

March 1963: Light and heater switch plate redesigned; rain drip molding added.

May 1963: Optional interior with Tenite woodgrain panels, woodgrain steering wheel, all black upholstery and "S-in-oblong" door panel ornaments.

June 1963: Tenite panels and woodgrain wheel phased in as standard equipment.

August 1963: Rear quarter-window latch redesigned, stronger hinge added to console box lid, console heater and air control handles given round instead of flat knobs, rubber doorsill plate redesigned, headlight bezels changed from round to square, parking lights restyled, grille added to radiator opening, hood support moved from left side to right, air intake grille added to left side of cowl (air duct to automatic transmissions on models without air conditioning), long battery replaced by standard-shaped battery, valve lifter cover (center valley plate) painted instead of chromed, inside air intake openings given plastic grilles, solid color interiors including black standard, inside door panel "S-in-oblong" emblems standard, rear window fastening again redesigned, pleated "Regal" vinyl upholstery replaced perforated Deluxe vinyl upholstery as standard, carpet color black only, fender plate changed to read Supercharged Avanti instead of Supercharged on R2 and R3.

September 1963: Electric window cable shield added to cable between body and door, manifold pressure gauge face redesigned, thicker padding added to bucket seat backs.

Price History
95+ point condition 1

	1982	1987	1990	Return
R1	$12,000	$17,500	$22,000	7.9%
R2	15,000	21,000	26,000	7.1
R3	16,000	23,000	28,000	7.2

R3 Avanti Production

Serial	Color	Transmission	Axle ratio
R5089	turquoise	four-speed	4.55
R5237	black	four-speed	4.55
R5394	white	four-speed	3.73
R5532	turquoise	four-speed	4.09
R5546	gold	four-speed	4.09
R5593	grey	automatic	4.09
R5625	black	automatic	unknown
R5642	white	automatic	unknown
R5643	white	automatic	unknown

Note: The last two cars were the final production Avantis, built in November 1963.

Chapter 28

Passenger Cars 1965–66

	Fun	Investment	Anguish
Daytona V–8	5	4	2
Other V–8s	3	3	2
Six-cylinder models	1	2	2

Unmistakable face of 1966: the final Studebakers, built at Hamilton, Ontario, and powered by Chevrolet. The facelift was the work of Bob Marcks, who more recently designed the Chrysler LeBaron convertibles for Lee Iacocca. It incorporated the traditional winged emblem and stand-up hood ornament with a handsome new rectangular pattern grille and dual headlamps instead of quads. This is a Daytona sports sedan.

Byers Burlingame, who relieved the ailing Egbert as Studebaker president in November 1963 and shut down South Bend one month later, has been unfairly pilloried as Studebaker's "undertaker." In fact, he tried to see a way out of the mess, meeting nonstop with the banks and investors and union, hoping for a miracle, finding none. After the axe fell on South Bend on December 9, Hamilton, Ontario, plant manager Gordon Grundy promised to carry on, but there was never any research and development, nor even an engineering or styling staff at Hamilton. It was nothing but a method to unload a few more cars, and to save face by a gradual phaseout rather than a complete closure in 1963.

These final Studebakers were good cars in many ways, and deserve their small but faithful collector following. With South Bend's foundry gone Hamilton had to find proprietary engines; Grundy obtained Chevrolet's 194 ci six (which Studebaker called the Skybolt) and its excellent 283 ci V-8 (which Studebaker called the Thunderbolt). The Chevrolet six was a major improvement on Studebaker's engine. Collectors argue more over the relative merits of the 283 and 289 small-block V-8s; of course the 283 came with none of the performance goodies previously found in the R Series engines, or for that matter, any of Chevy's hot-rod

For 1965, the Hamilton Studebakers were virtually unchanged in styling, although Chevrolet engines lurked under the hoods. New was a vinyl roof covering, available in either black or white; bucket seats were standard on Daytonas.

mods. It produced only 195 bhp, down 15–25 bhp from the previous Studebaker 289, and there was no power pack option.

There were no Avantis or Hawks in these final years, and the 1965s were carbon copies of the 1964 models on the outside. But a clever facelift by Bob Marcks' Detroit design firm of Marcks, Hazelquist, Powers transformed the 1966 model. Introduced for 1966 was flow-through ventilation (Refreshaire) with extractor vents above the taillights. Split-back reclining front seats and transistor ignition were standard on Daytonas, which continued to offer vinyl-covered roofs. Hamilton was pushing safety, and these 1966s came with dual padded sun visors, nonglare windshield wiper arms, dual master cylinder, padded dash, two-speed wipers, windshield washers, parking brake warning light, flanged rear axle shafts, safety door latches, and seatbelts front and rear. They also featured aluminized rust-proofing, a feature Studebaker should have had beginning in 1953. By this time, though, production was winding down rapidly, and barely 2,000 cars had been built for the 1966 calendar year before Grundy and Hamilton gave up.

What to Look For

The V-8 is far more preferable, from a collector standpoint, to the six, although the six is a fine engine. Daytona sport sedans are clearly the preferred models. In 1965 the six-cylinder Cruiser became available in North America for the first time since its reappearance in 1961, but this fact is only of academic significance. Disk brakes were standard on Daytonas, optional on the other models; four-speed manual gearboxes were not available.

Although there doesn't appear to be much of a value difference between the 1965 and 1966 model year, the 1966 is preferable on the grounds of both scarcity and interest: far fewer were built than 1965s, and the front-end facelift makes them appear distinctly different. The 1966 Daytona sport sedan is the preferred model, although collectors of rarity must consider the wagon production figures.

The 1965 Cruiser was offered in mass production for the first time with a six-cylinder engine. There was a minor change to Cruiser decklid moldings, which were made narrower than those on Daytonas this year.

Production

	1965	1966
Four-door sedans	10,239	5,686
Two-door sedans	7,372	2,321
Four-door wagons	1,824	940

Identification

For 1965: As per 1964 with Canadian-built McKinnon sixes and V-8s. Cruiser decklid moldings revised, wide decklid molding on Daytonas. For 1966: Single headlamps (probably the first time a manufacturer had gone *back* from quads as a styling gimmick); redesigned grille composed of four oblongs, blacked out on Daytona and Cruiser. Refreshaire flow-through ventilation with extractor outlets above taillights.

Specifications

Bodies: Two- and four-door sedans, four-door wagons.

Engines: Ohv six, 194 ci (3.56 x 3.25 in.), 120 bhp; ohv V-8, 283 ci (3.88 x 3.00 in.), 195 bhp.

The 1966 Daytona featured blacked-out grillwork; this V-8 carries a Hawk badge above the unorthodox numbers 283, which stood for the Chevrolet-built McKinnon small-block, Studebaker's 289 having been lost with the South Bend factory. Less than 2,500 two-doors were built in 1966, making them extremely scarce today.

Last of the last, Studebaker's 1966 Wagonaire, offered in a single series combining trim features of the Daytona and Commander and with either a fixed or sliding roof panel. Exterior trim followed that of the other 1966 models. Only 940 were built.

Chassis and drivetrain: Independent front suspension with coil springs and tubular shocks; live rear axle with semi-elliptic leaf springs.

Dimensions: Length 190 in. (two door), 194 in. (four door), 193 in. (wagons); wheelbase 109 in. (two door), 113 in. (four door/wagons); weight 2,695 lb. (Commander two door) to 3,070 lb. (Cruiser).

Serial Numbers

For 1965: six-cylinder C110001, V–8 C510001; 1966: six-cylinder C130001, V–8 C530001.

Price History

95+ point condition 1	1982	1987	1990	Return
Daytona V–8 sport sedan	$3,000	$3,800	$6,000	9.1%
V–8 wagons	3,250	4,250	6,000	8.0
V–8 sedans	2,250	3,000	5,000	10.5
Six-cylinder models	1,850	2,750	4,000	10.1

Chapter 29

Avanti II 1965–Current

	Fun	Investment	Anguish
1965–75 coupe	8	7	6
1976–90 coupe	8	3	9
1987 convertible	8	8	8

When the large South Bend dealership owned by Leo Newman and Nathan Altman was faced with the cessation of local Studebaker production, they tried to interest other manufacturers in taking on the Avanti. "I went to Checker in Kalamazoo, Michigan," Altman remembers. "Would you believe it? They said they'd never built a car as ugly as the Avanti! They build the Checker Marathon!"

Ultimately the partners bought the rights to the Avanti and a section of the abandoned plant and set up their own miniature production line, building what they called the Avanti II mainly by hand, using MFG fiberglass panels and Corvette engines. Cars were turned out virtually to order, and Altman wasn't above producing one in chartreuse and watermelon, if you wanted such a combination.

Production, such as it was, topped 100 in the good years, and while Altman was alive the Avanti II was an impressive car for such an unlikely operation. Touring the assembly

The 1969 Avanti II was still much in the image of the original, with mag-style wheels, covered headlamps (later banned by the government), side marker lights and driving lights.

These early IIs, such as this 1970 model, were beautifully executed under the firm hand of Nate Altman, who insisted on quality. After he died, quality vanished.

The 1974 Avanti II with an original solution to the Federal 5 mph bumper mandates.

line in the bleak South Bend mausoleum, one could hardly imagine a final product being turned out with such expertise. Altman made the Avanti II a success because he stayed with the original concept. The Federal government had to drag him kicking and screaming into 5 mph bumpers in 1973, for example.

Unfortunately, Altman died suddenly in 1976, and his successors mainly lacked his combination of salesmanship and love for the car. Avanti II quality sank. By the time construction tycoon Steve Blake bought the company in October 1982 the product was a bad joke: slow, clumsy, grossly trimmed in second-rate materials, with a paint job that made a Yugo look good and chrome plating you wouldn't accept on a Fiat. New switches had accumulated over the years, all of them seemingly controlled by identical toggle switches hidden under the dash. "Who the hell knows what they do?", Blake said in frustration during a 1983 interview.

Blake *did* love the car, and he seemed to know how to sell it. The 1983s were greatly improved and modified, with a new body-color bumper replacing the chrome (which few purists liked). He began designing a convertible, promising the workers success and riches if he succeeded. Improving quality was a good idea; the convertible was not, sapping Avanti's limited resources before the basic product was back on the tracks. In June 1985, Blake filed for bankruptcy.

A succession of managers then took over with little more to show for it, until Avanti Motors moved the operation lock, stock and barrel to Youngstown, Ohio. The convertible was deemphasized, management correctly concentrating on the coupe; but recently they have announced a thick-pillared, four-door sedan that simply looks like a bad dream.

Theoretically in the Avanti's market, you ought to be able to sell 400 or 500 copies a year of almost anything. But one notices that the only people who *do* are established manufacturers like Rolls-Royce or Ferrari. The replicar builders have never sustained that kind of volume. The Avanti is not quite a replicar, not quite a new car, but certainly a limited-edition car. Its appeal has never been to traditional car collectors, but to younger professional people. And those people nowadays are demanding.

What To Look For

The chief attraction of the Avanti II is its combination of the original style with greater luxury and, through 1975, superior workmanship. Some enthusiasts prefer the II for these reasons even though it is less "pure" (i.e., not all Studebaker) and has lower performance. Offsetting this is the switch to Chevrolet running gear, which makes the II a more practical choice for those who would rather enjoy their cars a lot on the road. The 327 V–8 used through 1970 is better in revving and running than the detoxed 350s and 400s; the new-generation 305 (1984) was a major improvement on both.

Avanti II workmanship deteriorated following Altman's death (especially paint, body and chrome finish), as did gas mileage under the weight of safety add-ons and emission controls. As the 1970s progressed, Avanti's solutions to meeting some requirements were of the backyard variety, notable in such areas as haphazard controls and jury-rigged air conditioners. Therefore, the 1965 models (which are considered prototypes) through

the 1969 are the best all-around choices, followed by the 1970–75 and the 1976–82 in that order.

The styling of the Blake-era cars (1983–85), with their thick-lip bumpers and flat black trim where the chrome ought to be, is a matter of personal preference. Blake replaced the original-style bumpers when a chrome expert told him it would cost $400 a pop to get a decent finish—but quantum design

People have just begun to get over the body-color bumpers Steve Blake put on the car in 1983 (whether they'll get over the plug-ugly 1990 four-door sedan is a separate question).

A late 1982 Avanti (no longer called the II) after the Blake takeover. This photo bears a handwritten note on the reverse: "New Avanti without rippled, orange peel or things falling off." Chrome wires were optional.

The carbureted GM 305 was a good-running V–8, and power rack-and-pinion steering was a powerful step forward; both items came with the new Blake management and this car. This is the special twentieth anniversary edition.

What Steve Blake called the 1984 "zowie interior": Recaro power buckets, padded leather dash top, cleaned-up switches and instruments, low-pile carpeting and an optional padded steering wheel. Build quality was now drastically improved, but at a price: Blake went bankrupt in 1985.

leaps on a body thirty years old rarely work. Blake insisted that the new bumpers were just bringing the Avanti up to date, ignoring the aesthetic principles they violated. (Would more people buy Avantis with the old chrome bumpers? Darned if I know, but they sure look a lot better.)

Some of Blake's other improvements, beginning with the 1983, were quite good. The General Motors carbureted 305 V-8 was a happier runner than the old LG4; power rack-and-pinion steering was a major improvement, as were the Recaro multi-adjustable seats and the fine audio equipment; the mystery toggle switches were eliminated. Of course, these recent Avantis cost a lot more, and exactly where they're going on the collector market is still unclear. The production convertible, which did appear briefly, would seem the best investment among Avantis of the 1980s.

One rather esoteric point about restoration: while most cars left South Bend with a fairly limited variety of color and trim combinations, a small number were built to order with some specific and, in some cases, bizarre equipment. Such a car presents obvious restoration problems; the flip side of this is that you need be relatively *less* concerned about originality with an Avanti II restoration, precisely because so few cars were built the same way. This opens up the prospect of being able to update the car with more modern equipment without detracting much from its handbuilt aura. You would never do that with an original Studebaker Avanti.

Production

For 1965, 45; 1966 59; 1967 66; 1968 100; 1969 92; 1970 117; 1971 107; 1972 127; 1973 106; 1974 123; 1975 125; 1976 156; 1977 146; 1978 165; 1979 142; 1980 168; 1981 195; 1982 188; 1983 276; from 1984-on, about 200 per year.

Price History

95+ point condition 1

	1982	1987	1990	Return
1965–75 Avanti II	$12,000	$16,000	$20,000	6.7%
1976–82 Avanti II		22,000	22,000	0.0
1983–85 Avanti coupe		35,000	25,000	–4.3*
1986–87 Avanti coupe			29,000	
1987 Avanti convertible			35,000	
1988 Avanti coupe			36,000	

*Negative return indicates depreciation.

Identification

Avanti II script from 1965; Avanti-style hood and rear roof quarter panels without S. For 1968: Side marker lights, clear at front. For 1969: Amber front marker lights, styled wheel option. For 1970: First year for Hurst four-speed option. For 1972: First year for turbo Hydra-matic. For 1973: New 400 ci V-8 and 5 mph bumpers. For 1975: Last year for four-speed option. For 1983: Body-color bumpers of box-section DuPont Kevlar. For 1984: Recaro power bucket seats, padded leather dash top cover, relocated switchgear, low-pile nylon carpeting; optional padded leather wheel. II eliminated from name. Package shelf trap door and passenger side vanity case eliminated. For 1985: GM 305 V-8; power rack-and-pinion steering. For 1987: Convertible introduced.

Specifications

Bodies: Two-door coupe (1965–date), two-door convertible (1987), four-door sedan (1990?).

Engines: Ohv V-8, 327 ci (4.00 x 3.25 in.), 300 bhp (1965–70); 350 ci (4.00 x 3.48 in.), 300 bhp (optional 1969–70), 270 bhp (1971–72); 210 net bhp (1976), 180 net bhp (1977–79), 190 bhp (1980–81), 200 bhp (1982–83); ohv V-8, 400 ci (4.13 x 3.75 in.), 245 bhp (1973), 180 net bhp (1974–75); ohv V-8, 305 ci (3.74 x 3.48 in.), 180 net bhp (1984), 205 net bhp (1985–87), 220 net bhp (1988–90).

Chassis and drivetrain: Independent front suspension, coil springs and tubular shocks; live rear axle with semi-elliptic leaf springs (1965–85); unequal length A-arms and coil springs front and rear (1986–date).

Dimensions: Length 192.5 in., wheelbase 109.1 in., weight 3,200 lb. (average).

Serial Numbers

Not available.

Chapter 30

Trucks 1902–64

Truck collecting is the fastest growing segment of the Studebaker scene today, spanning all eras from the 1930s to the 1960s. It is a recent development, which began to emerge in the mid to late 1970s.

Studebaker truck production began with small runabout Electrics in 1902, but early commercials of all kinds are rare. Larger Electrics with up to five-ton capacity were built in the early 1900s. But production was limited until after World War I. Then in the mid 1920s Studebaker began to produce ambulances, hearses and light-duty commercials in increasing volume. By 1929, Studebaker had several chassis available up to the Model 99 bus chassis of 184 in. In 1930 when Studebaker-Pierce-Arrow (SPA) Truck Corporation was organized, the S Series was announced, ranging from a half-ton delivery car to 160 in. wheelbase two-tons, produced through 1931. A larger three-ton model was added in 1931 as well as the Parlor Car chassis (Model 111) with a 220 in. wheelbase for bus use. Another 1932 commercial was the Rockne panel delivery.

Late in 1932, Studebaker purchased control of White to improve its truck business, but this liaison ended with the receivership of 1933. For 1934 the S Series yielded to the new T and W Series, which received minor restyling in 1935. For 1936 the big news was the Metro line of cab-forward trucks and, in 1937, the new J Series. The first diesel appeared in July 1927, the first K Series in 1938. Wheelbases up to 250 in. were offered for school buses by 1939.

The M Series dominated from its introduction in 1940 through early 1948, resulting in numerous desirable models, especially of half- to one-ton capacity. This was replaced with the 2R Series, laid out under chief truck engineer Russell MacKenzie and designed by Bob Bourke. The 2Rs were built in a special truck plant on Chippewa Avenue in South Bend, acquired from the War Assets Administration. Its essential lines lasted until the end of Studebaker production, but detail styling was altered beginning in 1954.

Truck production tapered down fast after Studebaker hit hard times in the mid 1950s; it had never been high, though the trucks

A 1905 Studebaker Electric with 2,500 lb. capacity, powered by two motors, each of 80 volts, would average 20–30 miles per charge. Larger Electrics with up to a five-ton capacity were also built.

A 1929 Erskine half-ton screen delivery owned by a Phoenix painter, from *Studebaker News*, July 8, 1929. I know of no Erskine trucks of any kind in existence—this would be quite a find.

A 1934 Big Chief model 1–W8–65 (165 in. wheelbase), nominally rated at three to four tons, with 358 ci Waukesha Hy-Powr 110 hp six. From the receivership period, these trucks were low-volume items and few, if any, have survived.

A 1938 K10 standard (narrow) express body on a Fast Transport chassis (essentially a one-ton pickup). A handsome example of the late prewar pickups designed by Loewy Associates.

are widely admired both for style and stamina. Peak production was 67,981 units in 1948.

What To Look For

It is difficult to pinpoint best buys among trucks because this is largely a matter of opportunity: condition is everything, and since truck chassis could be bought in a variety of configurations and adapted to numerous bodies supplied by outside firms, there is relatively less uniformity than among cars. Among ready-to-go, complete vehicles, the most popular are the 1960–64 Champ pickups, built as half- or three-quarter-ton only; the 1937–39 coupe-express; and all later V–8 powered big trucks because they are more capable in modern driving conditions.

Nor is it easy to assign values. Although increasingly popular, trucks were working vehicles, used hard when new and now in short supply. They hardly ever surface at auctions, but are traded instead among the committed enthusiasts—and sometimes money doesn't enter the transaction. The best place to look for Studebaker trucks is in the classified ads, and the most classifieds are published in *Turning Wheels*, the monthly magazine of the Studebaker Drivers Club.

Truck collector interest parallels Studebaker's most active period as a truckbuilder, and all models from runabouts to tractors are being restored, although the restoration work is often daunting. Prewar cab-over Metro models are the greatest challenge: they used extensive wood framing which took a terrific pounding in service, and they deteriorated fast. Those that survived until the 1940s largely fell victim to wartime scrap drives.

Condition is cruicial: after the M Series, which ended March 1948, Studebaker trucks were vulnerable to rust, and the Champ series is the worst of all. Replacement body panels are becoming scarce and new-old-stock is expensive, although Newman and Altman have offered some fiberglass fenders. Reproductions are increasingly available. The Packard Farm now makes excellent reproductions of C-cab floor mats, for example. Glass and interior components are on the increase.

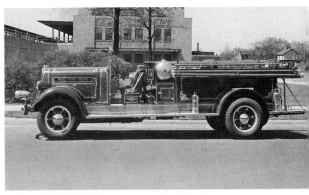

A 1938 K30 oil tanker from California (note the California-style headlights), probably the largest prewar Studebaker truck ever made. K30s had 900x20 tires, and some had full air brakes.

A beautiful 1938 Standard series Model K25 fire engine at South Bend Union Station. Much enthusiasm exists for fire apparatus restoration, including a special club: contact the Society for the Preservation and Appreciation of Antique Motor Fire Apparatus, PO Box 2005, Syracuse, NY 13220.

A striking paint job and whitewalls combine with Loewy's art deco styling on this rakish K10 panel from the 1938–40 period, being christened by Miss America (its namesake) and a bottle of Mumm's. By the time the war was over, most of these handsome prewar trucks had been run into the ground or lost in the scrap drives.

Another one that would be hard to find nowadays: the 1939 Standard series Model K20 tractor with vendor-supplied (or built) sleeper cab, rated at two to three tons, with Hercules JXB engine. Trailer, built by Edwards Iron Works of South Bend, was known as the Edwards Round Nose.

A fine piece of art deco design, Studebaker's 1936 model 2MB6 forward control bus chassis, with a twenty-two-passenger Metropolitan City body by FitzJohn Company, Muskegon, Michigan. The bus was photographed in service in Logansport, Indiana. Power was a Waukesha 6BM L-head six developing 78 hp. Some buses have been found and restored, but none of this type that we know of.

Model 2M–625 cab-over chassis with the Studebaker DeLuxe cab and half-yard Rex Concrete Mixer body; these two were operated by Tate Builders Supply in Covington and Dayton, Kentucky. Alas, chances are remote of finding such a period piece.

Predecessor to today's RVs? A great rig that would be a showstopper today is this1937 Model K20 tractor drawing what Studebaker called "the world's largest trailer." Designed to house four passengers plus a crew of "chauffeur and cook," the trailer featured a special "observation tower" for the passengers and sleeping, cooking and living quarters.

Model K20M cab-forward tractor with 101 in. wheelbase, pulling a trailer loaded with new 1939 Champions. The car trailer is beautifully styled in the art deco tradition. One of these today would be ideal for the serious meet-goer; some cab-forwards are in use for this purpose, but we've never seen one of these outstanding trailers.

A portent of trucking fifty years ahead, this K30 cab-forward is from the 1938–40 period. Tandem trailers are only now coming into popularity and must have seemed other-worldly in 1940.

The 1937 Coupe-Express half-ton Model J5, on a 116 in. wheelbase. This was the first year for the Coupe-Express, easily the most popular prewar Studebaker truck. The 1937 used all of the glamorous Loewy styling of concurrent passenger cars.

A 1938 Coupe-Express Model K5 on a 116.5 in. wheelbase. Loaded with accessories including an enclosed cargo area, the truck is equipped with overdrive, vacuum control, mohair seat, foglights, backup lights, radio, spotlight, rearview mirrors and bumper guards. Owner Harry Keller of Pasadena, California, sold children's dress goods. *Studebaker News*

The 1939 Coupe-Express Model L5 on a 116.5 in. wheelbase. Sought-after options on the Coupe-Express included spare tire with metal cover, rear bumper, bumper guards front and rear, Hill-Holder, overdrive, freewheeling, 7.00 and 6.50 tires, heavy-duty front springs, 4.82:1 rear axle ratio and demountable tarpaulin car-van top. Black was standard, other colors optional.

Popular neither at the time nor with today's collectors, the removable cargo box by Edwards Iron Works of South Bend was an accessory for Champion coupes in 1940. This photo shows a 1941 Champion, but the 1941 features have been airbrushed in; no Edwards pickups are known to have been fitted to 1941 models.

"Black-Out" model 1942 M15-20 one-ton pick-up, in wartime livery, with painted hubcaps, bumpers, headlight rims, grille and windshield frame, all of which had previously been chrome or stainless steel—materials that were in short supply after the United States entered World War II. These are extremely rare trucks; for example, there were only 314 half-tons, not all of which were Black-Outs. We know of four such trucks.

A Coke truck on the M16, 152 in. wheelbase chassis owned by Coca-Cola Bottling Company of South Bend. Introduced in 1941 (year of this model), the M Series was a handsomely designed series of trucks that would last Studebaker through the war and beyond.

Studebaker built the M29 Weasel throughout the war; this photo shows one in operator-training exercises. More Weasels are still available and running than prewar M Series trucks; quite a few are still in Europe. Several have been displayed at Studebaker Drivers Club national conventions.

Early production (probably 1941 or 1942) model US6-62 two-ton cargo truck; note characteristic squared-off fenders which contrast starkly with Studebaker cab. All military vehicles are collectible, but Studebakers are quite rare compared to, say, General Motors Corporation's. Close to 200,000 military Studebakers were built on a variety of wheelbases, but many were sent to allied armies and for lend-lease.

Extremely rare model M15–28 heavy-duty one-ton stake truck, the first truck produced by Studebaker for civilian use after the war—technically while the war was still on as production began in May 1945. Stakes were available only in Forest Green or Ruby Glow red and black; expresses began production in August, painted black with red wheels.

A 1946 M5–13 half-ton pickup, an early example because it still has painted headlamp rims and windshield, hood and grille moldings, black doorhandles and gas cap. Hubcaps are Studebaker, but not standard. A desirable model today.

The best-known postwar Studebaker pickups, 1949–53 2R Series replaced the M Series and was designed by Bob Bourke. The body stayed in place through the end of production, though refinements occurred as the years went by. Hood ornament was the same as used on passenger cars.

The 1954 3R three-quarter-ton pickup, with the first changes made to the R Series trucks since introduction: one-piece windshield, new grille and oval badges. Two-ton models were offered with a V-8 engine for the first time in domestic production.

The V-8 was made available on all trucks in 1955, which adopted a slightly new front end: integrated headlamps and parking lamps and new wider nameplate. Hood ornament was unique to trucks in 1955, reading S for sixes and 8 for V-8s; awnings over side windows were new and back window was much wider. In terms of performance, collectors prefer post 1954 V-8 half-tons for obvious reasons, and V-8 prices are higher.

Optional two-toning (probably red and black on this example), whitewalls and wheel covers on a good-looking 1956 model 2E7-122 half-ton. Again there was a front-end styling change: a scoop built into the hood and relocated parking lights. Transtar nameplate was first used on Studebaker trucks this year.

HA 1957 Model 3E7 Transtar DeLuxe half-ton V-8 pickup with 6 ft. box and optional two-toning, a combination that is much sought after by today's Studebaker truck collectors. New grille was fiberglass on 1957 models.

A 1958 Model 3E14-131 one-ton four-wheel-drive pickup being tested at the Studebaker Proving Grounds: just look at those axles going every which way, and the chassis with them! All truck frames were riveted together so that they would twist under terrain conditions like this.

139

Price-leading Scotsman Model 3E1-112 half-ton pickup, which was incredibly cheap at the $1,595 suggested retail price, was claimed to be the lowest-priced pickup in America. Work Star 185 ci six was the powerplant. Scotsmen were built during 1958–59 (Scots' plaid nameplate occurs on 1958s only) and were available with a wide variety of options, including V–8 and automatic.

Highly collectible, the 1963 Studebaker Zip Van was built for the United States Post Office and featured right-hand drive for rural delivery. Note radiator cap cover, a preproduction design.

The Champ pickups of 1960–64 are sought by many collectors. This is a 1961 Model 6E5-122 with wide box, showing the unique kick-up bright metal molding on the front fender, used only that year. Champ looks right up to date thirty years later, but the breed is rust-prone and good ones are hard to find.

Produce wholesaler Tony Mantia of Dayton, Ohio, ordered this handsome 1949 2R16-31 one and one-half-tonner, with box supplied by a specialty manufacturer.

A 1956 Model 2E38-131 two-ton tractor with 289 ci V-8 power and two-speed rear axle with Fruehauf trailer, operated by Homer Fitterling of South Bend, a notable car collector who amassed a famous fleet of Duesenbergs.

Built for the Marine Corps and believed used only on bases within the continental United States, this Model 8E 40C-171-C2 Transtar from 1963 is now owned by Asa Hall. Powered by the 289 V-8 with five-speed direct New Process transmission and single reduction rear axle, the truck used full air brakes. This vehicle was originally assigned to the base in Quantico, Virginia.

A 1962 Model 7E45E two-ton heavy-duty diesel tractor with optional flat-nose 96 BBC (bumper to back of cab) conversion. These trucks used a 4-53 Detroit diesel engine and featured full air brakes. The truck was one of ten such units delivered to a construction camp in Fort Wayne, Indiana.

Sources

Parts Suppliers

A&M Garage Inc.
2651 Webster Avenue
Bronx, NY 10458
Studebaker, Erskine, Rockne and Packard parts.

Antique & Classic Motorcars
Route 256
Imlaystown, NJ 08526
Specialist parts for Hawks, Larks and Avantis.

Brown Studebaker
818 Berlin Street
Mishawaka, IN 46544
New and used parts for postwar models and accessories.

Charles Conway
PO Box 102
Attleboro, MA 02703
Sales and service literature, back issue magazines and books; Studebaker specialist.

Mike Elling
1313 Crawford Street
Vicksburg, MS 39180
Reproduction rubber parts a specialty; other parts including new-old-stock.

Frost & French Inc.
230 East Avenue
Lancaster, CA 93535
Former dealership with large parts stock for Studebaker, especially late models.

Bruce Jones
6204 Bent Fork Circle
Raleigh, NC 27606
Postwar parts including new-old-stock and reproduction; literature, service, shop and owners manuals.

M&S Hydraulics
Antique Ford Shock Absorbers
18930 Couch Market Road
Bent, OR 97701
Shock absorbers for most postwar Studebakers.

Max Merritt
PO Box 27096
Indianapolis, IN 46227
Parts and accessories, new and reproduction.

Miller Studebaker Parts
PO Box 3493 University Station
Charlottesville, VA 22903
Hand-cast ½5 scale models.

Newman & Altman Inc.
405 West Sample Street
South Bend, IN 46634
Premier source of Studebaker parts, built around the factory's stock plus many reproduction parts including the essential postwar front fenders.

Packard Farm
97 North 150 West
Greenfield, IN 46140
An enormous array of Studebaker parts, including exhaust systems and body parts.

Patrician Industries
20408 Carlisle
Dearborn, MI 48124
Studebaker new-old-stock parts; door panels and upholstery a specialty.

Royal Gorge Studebaker
109 West Front
Florence, CO 81226
Engine and chassis rebuilding.

Charles Schnetiage
22136 Roscoe Boulevard
Canoga Park, CA 91304
Rubber, brake and mechanical parts; body trim parts including 1953–54 coupe script.

Steve's Studebaker-Packard
2287 Second Street
Napa, CA 94559
Parts and cars for sale.

Studebakers Only
1225 East Perry Road
Irving, TX 75060
Mechanical, sheet metal and trim.

Studebakers West
335A Convention Way
Redwood City, CA 94063
Wiring harnesses, suspension parts, engines, transmissions, superchargers; chassis and component rebuilding.

Total Performance Avanti
PO Box 168
Sebring, FL 33871
Offering accessories, parts and repair for performance Avantis.

Recommended Books

There are many Studebaker reference manuals, reprints of factory literature and collections of reprinted road tests. For a catalog including all of these write Classic Motorbooks, PO Box 1, Osceola, WI 54020. The following are books every Studebaker fan should have for their wealth of photos and accurate information.

Studebaker: The Complete Story, by Fred Fox and Bill Cannon. An outstanding model-by-model history by two experts on the subject, extensively illustrated and referenced, with appendices on detailed specifications, production figures, sales literature. 368 pages. Possibly out of print, but worth finding. Published at $39.95 by Tab Books Inc.

Bob Bourke Designs For Studebaker, by John Bridges. Until Don Vorderman of *Automobile Quarterly* (AQ) unearthed the true author of the glorious 1953–54 Starliner and Starlight, everyone called them the "Loewy coupes." Bourke told his story in *AQ* in 1971 and gained instant recognition, not only for those cars but for his many other fine designs over a career that spanned forty years. One of Bourke's fans, John Bridges, determined to put the story between hard covers. 198 pages. Published at $20 by J.B. Enterprises.

The Studebaker Century: A National Heritage, by Asa Hall and Richard M. Langworth. Hall's enormous photo collection is the basis of this photo-documentary: not a history, but a visual presentation of Studebaker's 100–plus years from the wagon days to the windup in Hamilton, Ontario, and the Avanti II. 192 pages, more than 700 photos. Published at $25.95. It is also available in deluxe, limited edition at $44.95 in padded leather with gilt page ends, page marker, numbered and signed by the authors from Dragonwyck Publishing Inc., PO Box 385M, Contoocook, NH 03229.

Studebaker: The Postwar Years, by Richard M. Langworth. Long out of print, a corporate history of the 1945–66 period summarizing both the product and the business end of things, through many interviews with former corporate heads, managers, designers and engineers. Difficult to find, try the antiquarian motorbookman, Tom Warth, Esq., Lumberyard Shops, Marine, MN 55047.

Recommended Magazines

Automotive Investor, 1651 Third Avenue, New York, NY 10128. Investment news, predictions, charts, photos, graphs and sales reports. Published monthly.

Car Collector, PO Box 171, Mount Morris, IL 61054. Slick monthly with feature articles, columns, color salons and a small number of ads.

Cars & Parts, PO Box 482, Sidney, OH 45365. Mostly ads, but with slick paper, feature articles and an interesting financial section. Published monthly.

Collectible Automobile, 7373 North Cicero Avenue, Lincolnwood, IL 60646. Glossy bimonthly, all color, with hardly any ads and packed with features.

Hemmings Motor News, PO Box 100, Bennington, VT 05201. A telephone-book-size monthly chock-full of information on cars, parts and services.

Old Cars Weekly, 700 East State Street, Iola, WI 54990. The hobby newspaper, also with many ads.

Skinned Knuckles, 175 May Avenue, Monrovia, CA 91016. The premier magazine on auto restoration, with well-illustrated articles and columns.

Special-Interest Autos, PO Box 196, Bennington, VT 05201. Glossy bimonthly on non-classic, non-antique collector cars, heavy on Studebakers.

Owners Clubs

All Studebaker owners or admirers should join the Studebaker Drivers Club, PO Box 3044, South Bend, IN 46619. This is the oldest and largest Studebaker club. It is professionally staffed, has a five-figure membership and publishes a thick monthly publication, *Turning Wheels.* The latter contains a profusion of classified ads for cars, parts and services. The Studebaker Drivers Club is absolutely indispensable to all Studebaker enthusiasts and has been for a long time.

The Antique Studebaker Club, PO Box 28845, Dallas, TX 75228. Numbers 900 members devoted to all Studebaker vehicles through the 1946 model year and M Series trucks through 1948. They publish a bimonthly magazine and a roster.

The Avanti Owners Association International, PO Box 28788, Dallas, TX 75228. A well-established specialty club for Avanti owners, with an excellent journal and strong organization.

Studebaker National Museum

Not many makes of car have their own museums. This one took a long time to establish, but quickly acquired donations of cars and memorabilia when it did, and is now one of the musts among transport museums in the United States. A mecca for Studebaker admirers, the museum displays Studebaker vehicles from the earliest horsedrawn wagons to prototypes of cars that never were and also offers an excellent library in the Studebaker Corporation Archival Collection. The Museum is located at 520 South Lafayette Boulevard, South Bend, IN 46601.